PROJECT ON NATIONAL SECURITY REFORM

VISION WORKING GROUP REPORT AND SCENARIOS

Sheila R. Ronis
Editor

July 2010

The views expressed in this report are those of the authors and do not necessarily reflect the official policy or position of the Department of the Army, the Department of Defense, or the U.S. Government. Authors of Strategic Studies Institute (SSI) publications enjoy full academic freedom, provided they do not disclose classified information, jeopardize operations security, or misrepresent official U.S. policy. Such academic freedom empowers them to offer new and sometimes controversial perspectives in the interest of furthering debate on key issues. This report is cleared for public release; distribution is unlimited.

*****

This publication is subject to Title 17, United States Code, Sections 101 and 105. It is in the public domain and may not be copyrighted.

*****

The Vision Working Group of the Project on National Security Reform began its efforts in December 2005 when the Honorable James R. Locher III, soon to be the Project's Executive Director, met with the author and Robert B. Polk and Daniel R. Langberg of the Institute for Defense Analyses to discuss the urgent need for national security reform. The mission of the overall Project was clear—rewrite the National Security Act of 1947 along with the associated Presidential Directives and Executive Orders required to put in place a U.S. national security system for the 21st century.

Over time, all of the Working Groups would receive mandates and specific study guidance. This volume is a compilation of some of the Vision Working Group processes and products that were used to inform the larger study, based upon work done over a 3-year period. It is a companion document to the overall study, *Forging A New Shield,* released on December 2, 2008, and available to download from *www.pnsr.org*. Robert B. Polk and Daniel R. Langberg served as my deputies until this past year.

*****

No effort of this size can be made without the contributions of many people. My colleagues in the Project's Executive Secretariat were crucial in our efforts, Jim Locher, Chris Lamb, Kate Yates, and Carrie Madison. Brian Helmer, who joined us in the last year, along with Steve Johnson, were extremely supportive. In addition, my colleagues on the leadership team who helped us immeasurably include Charlie Stevenson, Myra Shiplett, John Bordeaux, Kath Hicks, Dan Gerstein, Richard Weitz, David Berteau, Erik Leklem, Vikram Singh, Limor Ben-Har, and Kori Schake. Members of our guiding coalition who deserve special mention in support of the Vision Working Group efforts are Leon Fuerth, whose patience and teachings are incalculable, especially his concepts of "anticipatory governance and forward engagement"; Brent Scowcroft, whose overall guidance for several years has been essential to our success; and Tom Pickering, who accurately provided the Guiding Coalition with a description of our preliminary work.

Members of the Vision Working Group who each provided separate and distinct support and guidance include Jim Burke,

Bill Doll, Joe Gueron, Erik Kjonnerod, David Leech, John Meagher, Carmen Medina, Matthew Russell, Chris Waychoff, Hans Binnendijk, Brad Botwin, David Couzens, Paul Halpern, Paul Hanley, Rudy Lohmeyer, Andy Marshall, and Elton "Thumper" Parker. Research Fellows to the Vision Working Group include Marcello Abbruzzeti, Lindsey Gehrig, Ian Grant, and Mary Shea. Other research support was provided by Bob Wysocki, Myron Stokes, Doug Orton, Trudi Lang, James McHann, Jon Stoffel, Matthew Schmidt, and Chris Wasden. This volume was developed with the support of Caylan Ford, my graduate research assistant, and Richard Chasdi, my new deputy.

The scenarios we produced would not be as robust as needed were it not for Lieutenant General Frances C. Wilson, USMC, President, The National Defense University, whose permission to work with the three Commandants of The National War College, Major General Robert P. Steel, U.S. Air Force; The Industrial College of the Armed Forces, Rear Admiral Garry E. Hall, U.S. Navy; and the Joint Forces Staff College, Major General Byron S. Bagby, U.S. Army; and their national security faculty improved the scenarios immensely. We are grateful to them all.

The scenarios also could not have been developed without the extensive assistance of the National Academies and Patricia S. Wrightson, Ph.D., Director, Committee on Scientific Communication and National Security, Policy and Global Affairs Division, who hosted our conference with the scientists who began our process. We also wish to thank Lieutenant General Brent Scowcroft and Dr. John Hennessy, the co-chairs of the Committee on Scientific Communication and National Security (CSCANS) at the National Academies who supported our efforts.

My work with the Project could not have occurred without the steadfast support of President Stephanie W. Bergeron and Dr. Robert L. Minter, Chief Academic Officer of Walsh College, and their understanding of the critical work of the Project to the nation and the world.

One member of the Vision Working Group who merits special attention is Patti Benner. Her intellectual guidance and perseverance enabled us to think more clearly about the entire assignment, and I am very grateful to her.

Last, but not least, I wish to thank the Strategic Studies Institute (SSI) and the U.S. Army War College, particularly, Dr. James Pierce, SSI Director of Publications, and his support staff, Ms. Rita Rummel, Mr. Richard J. T. Juday, and Mrs. Jennifer E. Nevil for their editorial and graphics support.

Sheila R. Ronis, Ph.D.
Vision Working Group Leader
September 2009
Washington, DC

Core Contributors
Sheila Ronis, Editor
Lauren Bateman
Jim Burke
Richard Chasdi
Caylan Ford
Lindsey Gehrig
Emily Hawkins
Trudi Lang
Daniel R. Langberg
Carrie Madison
John Meagher
Robert B. Polk
James Douglas Orton
Matthew Russell
Chris Waychoff

Research Contributors

Of the 133 experts who participated in building timelines into the future, the following individuals gave permission for PNSR to use their names and affiliations. Dozens wished to remain anonymous.

Timothy D. Leuliette, Chairman, Dura Automotive Systems
Dianne Bommarito, Manager, Advanced Technology Process
    Group, General Motors Corporation
Jacques S. Gansler, University of Maryland
Bette Moen, Cedar Crest Academy
Harry Kesten, Cornell University (Emeritus)
Lewis M Branscomb, University of California San Diego, and
    Harvard University (Emeritus)
Timothy Mack, World Future Society
Dr. Terry Feagin, Professor of Computer Science, University of
    Houston - Clear Lake
Desineni Subbaram Naidu, Idaho State University

Gerald Abbott, Industrial College of the Armed Forces, National Defense University
Stephen E. Fienberg, Carnegie Mellon University
Roger George, Global Futures
Nadine G. Barlow, Ph.D., Northern Arizona University
Michael Norton, Department of Chemistry, Marshall University
E. H. Brown, Independent (previously government subcontractor for investigations)
Kenneth I. Berns, University of Florida Genetics Institute
David Cole, Chairman, Center for Automotive Research
Ian A. Paul, Ph.D., University of Mississippi Medical Center
Gerald Lushington, University of Kansas
Maher S. Amer, Wright State University
Michael Mascagni, Florida State University
J. David Patterson, Principal Deputy Under Secretary of Defense (Comptroller)
Major Goodman, NC State University
Andrew Fire, Stanford University
E. A. Hammel, University of California, Berkeley
Walther N. Spjeldvik, Physics Department, Weber State University
Dr. Robert Frederking, Carnegie Mellon University
Ivan R. King, University of Washington
Ronald Coifman, Yale University
Michael Kalichman, Research Ethics Program, University of California, San Diego
Elizabeth F. Loftus, University of California, Irvine
Paul Roepe, Georgetown University
Dr. Carolyn D. Heising, Professor of Industrial, Mechanical and Nuclear Engineering, Iowa State University of Science and Technology
Takahiro Hiroi, Brown University
Mike Zaworotko, University of South Florida
Roy H. Doi, University of California, Davis
Aftab A. Ansari, Emory University School of Medicine

Additional thanks also go to:

Harold M. Agnew
Kenneth J. Arrow
William B. Bridges
Martin Buoncristiani
King-Thom Chung

Michael Freeling
Dr. C. T. Hess
Christopher T. Hill
E. Leonard Jossem
William Kemperer
V. Ramanathan
Richard Weitz
Dr. James K. Wyatt
Mingqing Xiao
Northrop Grumman
University of California, Berkeley
University of Michigan
Massachusetts Institute of Technology

*****

Comments pertaining to this report are invited and should be forwarded to: Director, Strategic Studies Institute, U.S. Army War College, 122 Forbes Ave, Carlisle, PA 17013-5244.

*****

All Strategic Studies Institute (SSI) publications may be downloaded free of charge from the SSI website. Hard copies of this report may also be obtained free of charge by placing an order on the SSI website. The SSI website address is: *www.StrategicStudiesInstitute.army.mil*.

*****

The Strategic Studies Institute publishes a monthly e-mail newsletter to update the national security community on the research of our analysts, recent and forthcoming publications, and upcoming conferences sponsored by the Institute. Each newsletter also provides a strategic commentary by one of our research analysts. If you are interested in receiving this newsletter, please subscribe on the SSI website at *www.StrategicStudiesInstitute.army.mil/newsletter/*.

ISBN 1-58487-452-X

CONTENTS

Foreword ix

Précis xi

Introduction xv
    Leon Fuerth

1. The Center for Strategic Assessment
   and Analysis 1
       Sheila R. Ronis and Caylan Ford

2. Scenario Use in the Project on National
   Security Reform 23
       Sheila R. Ronis

3. The Pre-Reform Nine Scenarios 37
       *Chris Waychoff, Matthew Russell, John Meagher,
   and Jim Burke*

4. The Nine Post-Reform Scenarios 79
       Chris Waychoff and Matthew Russell

5. A Defense Industrial Base Scenario 105
       Sheila R. Ronis

6. Nuclear Bomb Case Study 139
       *Lindsey Gehrig, Lauren Bateman,
   and Sheila R. Ronis*

Appendix A: Stress Testing Results 179

Appendix B: Using Scenario-Based Planning
to Develop a Vision of Success 187

About the Contributors 251

FOREWORD

On November 26, 2008, the Project on National Security Reform submitted its 2-year study of the national security system, *Forging a New Shield*, to the President, President-elect, and Congress. The study found that the national security system was at risk of failure and needed serious reform. Before the Project finalized the report's recommendations, its Vision Working Group tested the findings against a diverse set of scenarios to determine if the recommendations were robust and effective. This testing revealed that each of the five major findings improved the performance of the current national security system. This volume documents the scenario-testing process used by the Vision Working Group. It includes the actual pre-reform and post-reform scenarios and details many other scenario techniques used in the overall study.

The work of the Vision Working Group has led to the formulation of another recommendation: The country must establish a mechanism to infuse greater foresight into the Executive Branch, and in particular the national security system. This proposed mechanism, named the Center for Strategic Analysis and Assessment, would exist and operate within the Executive Office of the President. This volume details the proposed architecture and operation of the Center.

The Project on National Security Reform advocates establishment of such a foresight mechanism as part of the larger transformation of the national security system and is ready and willing to assist in its implementation.

JAMES R. LOCHER III
President and CEO
Project on National Security Reform

PRÉCIS

Creating an organization dedicated to the promotion of societal vision would appear to be a contradiction in terms. Vision is fundamentally an individual characteristic, and a rare one at that. The ability to see beyond widely accepted forms and to think beyond conventional limits is a trait that is not widely distributed. Nor is it always valued. Vision is not widely welcomed in organizations, since these exist primarily to promote standardized, collective behavior. Within these systems, those who manifest a talent for vision are at risk of being isolated rather than accepted.

All truly new ideas destroy what they replace. However, sooner or later, what was once new and radical becomes what is established and orthodox. And orthodoxy seeks to perpetuate itself. The process of scanning the horizon for the next great news must be continuous, and never bound to conceptions of "permanent" truth.

Until recently, we studied the past to learn how to survive in the future. That is the hallmark of the academic mind. However, experience shows that if the past is taken too literally, it ceases to be a guide to the future and instead becomes a cul-de-sac. Today, we are struggling to come to grips with societal issues that are powerful, fast-moving, and complex. This is a combination that can overwhelm seemingly powerful organizations, thought to be operating on the basis of well-tried principles.

Because of an excessive reliance on previously successful patterns, great American corporate names have vanished, and others barely cling to existence. The same can most definitely apply to nations; witness the disappearance of the Soviet Union. If we do not take care, it can apply to the United States as well.

Survival depends on agility, and agility depends upon the capacity to adjust behavior correctly, under conditions where time for perception is contracting. In human affairs, it is not possible to predict the future; but it is possible to study alternative futures and in the process become more prepared for a range of contingencies, and gain time for organizations to prepare to deal successfully with surprise.

The Project on National Security Reform (PNSR) is an effort to promote these characteristics by developing a more effective network within government to manage challenges to national security. In that sense, it is a continuation of work initiated by the Goldwater-Nichols Act, which began a reorganization of the national security process that is still underway within the Department of Defense.

But it is much more than that. What PNSR seeks to do is to inspire a whole-of-government approach to fundamental changes in the nature of the scope of the challenge to national security.

It is no longer possible to conflate national security and national defense. A powerful uniformed military able to defeat the armed forces of any state is not necessarily able to provide, in and of itself, for the security of the nation. We see ever more clearly that national security is the product of a larger system of capabilities—extending far beyond formal military power. Among these assets is the ability to tolerate—in fact to encourage—the exploration of unorthodox visions of what may come: the better to prepare for decision-making in the presence of uncertainty.

One might think that it is the mission of the intelligence community to provide this service. The function of intelligence services, however, is to reduce uncertainty through the discovery and analysis of patterns that might otherwise be concealed. Something else is needed, however, in the form of a system that exists to increase uncertainty, by expanding rather than reducing the number of possible futures that can be identified and analyzed. Only in this way is it possible to test and learn about the consequences of possible actions, by studying and perfecting them first in the mind's eye, rather than putting them to the ultimate and irreversible test in the field.

PNSR's Vision Working Group has devoted itself to the study of contingencies operating at the societal level. Its recommendations, presented in this book, present the case for "vision" as the output of a continuous, organized process, at the service of the highest levels of government, embracing both civilian and military concerns and perspectives. It also makes the case for creating an institutional setting for this process, in the form of the proposed Center for Strategic Analysis and Assessment.

The proposed Center for Strategic Analysis and Assessment is a way to square the circle: to build an organization that serves national security for the future by challenging the very ideas upon which it is based in the present. It reflects a basic truth: that there is no riskier approach to national security than building it on the assumption that the future is a linear extension of the past. The Law of Unintended Consequences is, ultimately, not a metaphor but a precise statement of the human condition. Continuity is an illusion; and change is our reality. Predictability is a chimera; but probability is a guide to humility in the presence of irreducible unknowns.

It is particularly important that the proposal for a Center for Strategic Analysis and Assessment also locates this entity in the Office of the President. Fragments of such a system exist in various parts of the

Federal Government. But no single system exists for the application of foresight to governance as a whole. Moreover, the place where this capability is most critically needed is as close to the President as possible.

Our political system depends on the wide dispersal of talent and initiative throughout the nation. The American people do not stand around waiting for Washington to tell them what to do. But they do depend on Washington to act as a wise agent on their behalf. Above all, they depend on the President to speak for their needs and their beliefs. The presidency is where power and vision come to their sharpest focus: the one office whose incumbent is fully entitled to speak for the nation as a whole by articulating its hopes in the form of vision for the future. In the Old Testament's Book of Proverbs, it is written, "Where there is no vision, the people perish."[1] The Report of the Vision Working Group is a reminder of this warning.

LEON FUERTH
The Project on Forward Engagement
Washington, DC
www.forwardengagement.org

ENDNOTES - PRÉCIS

1. Christian Bible, Old Testament, American King James Version, Book of Proverbs 29:18.

INTRODUCTION

The Project on National Security Reform's (PNSR) December 2008 report, *Forging a New Shield*,[1] represents the culmination of nearly 3 years of intellectual work by more than 300 dedicated national security executives, professionals, and scholars. The report provides a thorough historical analysis of the current U.S. national security system, evaluates its capabilities and performance, and proposes a comprehensive reform agenda to prepare the system to meet the challenges and opportunities of the 21st century.

This publication will describe the Vision Working Group's efforts to stress test the solution sets proposed in *Forging a New Shield* and will showcase several of the scenarios developed for the Project, exemplifying processes that need to be permanently housed in a "whole of government" Center in the Executive Office of the President.

Chapter 1 looks in detail at the major finding of the Vision Working Group: the need for the nation to have capabilities for looking to the future and the creation of the Center for Strategic Analysis and Assessment in the Executive Office of the President.

Chapter 2 describes the methodology that was used to create the scenarios. PNSR chose to develop and use scenarios to see if the recommendations created performed better than the current system. This chapter also describes the stress testing process and the lessons learned by the Project's team.

Chapter 3 includes the nine pre-Project on National Security Reform (PNSR) scenarios that were developed for and used by the PNSR staff to stress test the Project's recommendations.

Chapter 4 includes the post-PNSR reform scenarios illustrating how different the outcomes of events would be with the PNSR reforms implemented.

Chapter 5 includes an example of another process needed within a new Center in the Executive Office of the President, a "future case study scenario" used to think through issues related to the U.S. industrial base supply chain for weapon systems and the country's dependence on China for many products that find their way into weapon systems whether acknowledged or not.

Chapter 6 addresses still another process needed within the new Center based on an "analytical case study" example that explores many issues regarding the possibility of a nuclear device detonated within the United States and the issues we need to consider today.

Finally, this publication includes two appendices. Appendix A provides the stress testing results of our findings. Appendix B includes a problem analysis of the reasons why scenarios have not found widespread use in the national security system to date.

ENDNOTES - INTRODUCTION

1. *Forging a New Shield*, Arlington, VA: Project on National Security Reform, 2008.

CHAPTER 1

THE CENTER FOR STRATEGIC ASSESSMENT AND ANALYSIS

Sheila R. Ronis
Caylan Ford

The United States began with a vision of a future world and the role our Founding Fathers hoped to create for themselves and their country. It was articulated in the Declaration of Independence, culminating decades of debate by the colonies' leading thinkers. What they wanted to do had never been done before. No colony had ever broken off from its parent country in the history of the world, nor established a democratic system premised on protecting the values of equality and freedom. But Thomas Jefferson and his Declaration Committee knew that it was the future they wanted for themselves and their fellow citizens. They knew it would be a difficult journey, and they knew it would be an experiment. They also knew that the vision they described in their Declaration would change their future. They could not have known how much it would also change the world.

Well over 200 years have since elapsed, and the Founding Fathers' vision of a strong, prosperous, and free nation still resonates. Yet the very challenges that would seek to undermine this vision have evolved. Indeed, since the signing of the National Security Act in 1947, threats to the United States have grown increasingly complex and multifaceted, and change now occurs at a vastly accelerated rate. These shifts necessitate that the nation once again look to the future, and prepare to meet a world that is very different from the one we have known.

Today, many of the most pressing challenges to the United States do not take the form of strong and aggressive states. Instead, they include diverse threats, including nonstate actors, environmental change, pandemic disease, recession, a burgeoning national debt, and so on. Addressing such disparate challenges demands a range of capabilities and expertise.

The authors of *Forging a New Shield* note, for instance, that success in Iraq and Afghanistan will require a combination of diplomacy, intelligence, law enforcement, economic development, and military tools. Similarly, achieving energy security will require integration of economic, science and technology, military, and intelligence policies, if not more.[1] To complicate matters, it must be understood that the global environment in which we exist is a complex system. As described by Leon Fuerth, former national security advisor to Vice President Al Gore, complex problems "do not lend themselves to permanent solutions, but instead morph into new problems, even as the result of our interventions to deal with them. They do not automatically tend towards stable outcomes, but may exhibit highly disproportionate consequences in response to relatively small changes of conditions."[2] Mr. Fuerth also stated that:

> We have attained the capacity to rapidly advance industrial civilization to new heights or to abruptly end it, with a diminishing margin of error between these two outcomes. Nuclear energy and nuclear war. Globalization of wealth, and global depression. Genetic interventions for the relief of hunger and disease, and genetic interventions running out of control, guided exclusively for profit or for war. Sustainable industrial civilization, or irretrievable environmental disorder. The polarities are very extreme, and thus the need for anticipatory governance is acute.[3]

Adapting to this increasingly complex environment thus necessitates not only that we improve the system's ability to communicate across a horizontal range of competencies, but also that it learn to *anticipate* the potential future impacts of changes to the system and respond to unanticipated events.

The Project on National Security Reform has proposed a series of reforms that would equip the U.S. Government to better meet and respond to this new security environment we inhabit. These include a proposal for the creation of a strategy cell within the National Security Council Staff, which would serve to improve strategic planning and assist in linking resources to strategy. In addition, plans are in development to help create the necessary incentives and infrastructure to support greatly improved information sharing and cooperation across all agencies, thus facilitating future responses to any and all contingencies.

Yet a vital capability gap remains. As of now, the country still has no capacity to construct a holistic understanding of the global and national security landscape that we inhabit nor do we have the ability to anticipate what lies ahead into medium- and long-term time frames. Because of the limited scope of issues traditionally understood to be germane to national security, and the inability to see beyond the terms of 2 to 4 years, the system can be said to suffer from both tunnel vision and near-sightedness.

An apt analogy would be to view the country as a car, speeding along a highway at 90 mph in a thick fog, which can be penetrated only a short distance by the headlights. The car may be well assembled and highly responsive, with its parts well oiled. Its driver might be exceptional, and he may know exactly where he wants to end up. But if he does not know the road that lies ahead, all would be for naught. It is only a matter of time before he, robbed of sight, becomes lost before he misses his turn, or worse.

The system needs to be able to see the road ahead. It must be aware of the hazards in its path, and be able to self-correct in the event of unanticipated difficulties. It must also be able to anticipate where a particular turn will take it, not only immediately, but also farther down the road. In other words, it needs the equivalent of a global positioning system (GPS).

To fulfill this function, the Vision Working Group proposes the establishment of a Center for Strategic Assessment and Analysis (CSAA) within the Executive Office of the President. The role of the Center will be to continually scan the future, ranging from what lies immediately ahead to what looms well in the distance. It will assess the relationships among the many moving parts that comprise the international political, social, technological, economic, and security landscape, and appraise the possible future ramifications of various policy alternatives. The Center will produce reports assessing a range of possible futures, providing a view into the risks, threats, and opportunities ahead. In doing so, the Center will help policymakers determine which courses of action to pursue and which to avoid in order to arrive at the most desirable future. Moreover, the Center will build and continually update hundreds of small-scale scenarios involving specific contingencies, and maintain dozens of 360-degree scenarios that provide holistic views of possible future worlds. By maintaining such a vast database of scenarios, the center will be able to instantly provide policymakers with a pool of knowledge to reference in the event of emergent crises. For instance, the center might run scenarios concerning the collapse of the North Korean regime, including the possible effects on U.S. stabilization and aid efforts. In other words, the Center will be able to tell policymakers, in real time, what the probable impacts of proposed responses would be.

In effect, the Center will provide the information necessary to enable the nation's leaders to develop "grand strategy" — defined by Martha Crenshaw as "a more inclusive conception that explains how a state's full range of resources can be adopted to achieve national security. It determines what the state's vital security interests are, identifies critical threats to them, and specifies the means of dealing with them."[4]

RAND analyst Bruce Don suggests that, at a basic level, governments must take several fundamental measures to develop competence in responding to complex and unpredictable systems: first, policymakers should look at a range of possible futures, rather than betting on a single outcome. Competing experts and agencies must be brought onto the same page, such that they understand the environment they are operating in and the convergences of their interests. Policies must be designed to hedge against undesirable outcomes, to adapt to change, and to learn amidst it, and the robustness of policies must be rigorously and constantly assessed.[5]

The CSAA will serve precisely these functions, allowing policymakers to consider a range of possible futures, and serving as a venue in which to test the possible future effects of policy options. This is not to say that the Center will possess predictive capacities. As explained by Yehezkel Dror, "All deep drivers of history are undergoing radical transformation, including population quantities and compositions, power structure, cultures and value systems, probably climate, and more. Ergo, within the 21st century many features of reality will take forms inconceivable at present."[6]

This reality means that no one is capable of accurately envisioning the future. But it also means that more than ever, we must try. We must develop greater foresight and awareness of the path we are on, of the consequences of our decisions, and of the major challenges that await us ahead. Doing this involves, in part, the continuous development and exploration of future scenarios to enhance our preparedness and improve our chances of success. To that end, this product by the Vision Working Group contains multiple examples of scenarios as a demonstration of what this capacity can look like.

If this goal is to be achieved, the United States will move from merely reacting to emergencies to pre-empting them, from responding to threats to seizing opportunities. It will make it possible to preserve the values, freedoms, security, and global leadership of the United States in the 21st century. Failure to act, however, could mean that the nation is caught off-guard by emerging threats, unable to see them until they have become imminent and, perhaps, intractable problems. In the worst case, the country could suffer what has been described as a synchronous failure, wherein the adaptive capacity of government and society is overwhelmed by the convergence of diverse and interacting stresses, resulting in a breakdown of institutional and social order.

SCOPE

Time Frames.

As the rate of change and the complexity of challenges continue to increase, there is little doubt concerning the value of conducting forward-thinking strategic planning and attempting to foster a more anticipatory government. However, the turnover and shifts in priorities that accompany successive administrations can render this process difficult. Long-term planning, to the extent that it has been attempted, is limited to some 2 to 4 years out, and strategies, structures, and processes that take longer to achieve may be discarded by future administrations or congresses.

The Center for Security Analysis and Assessment will seek to provide a consistent basis for the creation of forward-thinking national strategy. This is to be accomplished by providing both near- and long-term projections and visions of the global environment extending well beyond the time frame of one administration. These projections will be continually assessed and revised, but will retain the characteristics of incorporating all facets of national power. The work of the center will thus help inform the policies of each new administration. It will also help minimize the risk of presidents pursuing policies that produce unintended adverse consequences for future administrations to grapple with.

Issues and Competencies.

No extant or proposed strategic planning centers within the national security system are capable of encompassing the full range of issues that impact national security. This is due, in part, to the need to limit to a manageable level the mandates of our national security and federal apparatus. To permanently and dramatically expand the scope and participation of the National Security Council, for instance, is neither feasible nor desirable; it would risk casting too wide a net, rendering the organization too ponderous to efficiently devise and implement policies.

And yet these capabilities must exist, as the national security environment is a complex system whose interacting variables cannot be understood when broken down into component parts, but must be looked at as a whole.

The CSAA will seek to provide a holistic understanding of the national security environment in order to produce visions of possible futures. The center will reflect this understanding by broadening the traditional conceptions of where to draw on talent intrinsic to the process of public policy formulation. It will reach out to include insights from academia and the private sector to include experts in several functional and regional fields, incorporating a diverse range of competencies and expertise spanning all major elements of national power.

THE ROLE OF THE CENTER FOR SECURITY ANALYSIS AND ASSESSMENT

The role of the center is not to create or dictate policy. Rather, its goal is to provide a context and analytical basis to facilitate the development of forward-looking strategy. The center would support the national planning process and develop a common view of the national security system as well as a common view of the external environment that encompasses space, global issues, regions, specific countries, and U.S. domestic trends. It will provide policymakers with an understanding of the range of possible futures they face, and enable them to see areas of convergence and overlap among departments.

The center can, at the request of the president, the National Security staff, or any other interagency task force, utilize the tools at its disposal to assist in the formulation of grand strategy. It may also examine specific questions where the impact and solutions transect multiple government agencies and have long-term implications. The primary intended audience of the center's work is the president himself, although he may task the center to report to the national security advisor, the vice president, or the chief of staff.

The Center for Security Analysis and Assessment can research, assess, or game any issue presented to it that fits the following criteria:

- Interagency problems requiring multidisciplinary systemic and strategic approaches.
- Issues with long-term strategic implications, either in foreign or domestic spheres.
- Issues of national or global importance with policy or strategic implications.

The findings and publications produced by the center will be made available across the interagency to assist in the development of robust policies and grand strategy.

CAPABILITIES, FUNCTIONS, AND TOOLS

Rigorous Analysis and Testing.

The Center for Security Analysis and Assessment will be uniquely positioned to provide rigorous research, analysis, and testing of policy ideas and proposed solution sets, as it will command substantial research resources, leading-edge technologies, and gaming capabilities.

Effective policies must be grounded in rigorous analysis incorporating both a multidisciplinary approach as well as sensitivity to the ways in which policies will affect other variables. Failing that, policies may be made based on false or outdated assumptions or may produce adverse unintended consequences in the long term.

Currently, the various organizations of the Federal Government are host to exceptional bodies of knowledge and expertise. Yet our ability to engage in rigorous analysis in crafting policies is hindered by an inability to bring together these diverse competencies to develop a holistic understanding of the national security environment.

Moreover, the various agencies lack the resources, time, and sometimes the expertise to thoroughly test the assumptions of analysts, which may prove false, outdated, or incomplete. The Center for Security Analysis and Assessment will seek to remedy these shortcomings. Unburdened by the need to make or implement policy or to engage in crisis management, it is wholly devoted to problem analysis, research, scenario development, contingency planning, gaming, and assessment.

While the center will not be involved in creating policy, it will offer the tools to engage in forward-looking assessment of the global national security environment, thus providing a valuable context for the President and the interagency to devise strategy.

In addition to leveraging human intellectual capital, the center will house leading-edge technologies and tools to assist in creating visions of the future. These may include computer capabilities to model possible interactions and future scenarios, and display capabilities designed to identify critical variables and the complex links tying disparate factors together. It will be capable of carrying out research in both secure and non-secure environments, according to the system's needs.

Assessment and Visioning.

The Center's process begins by building an understanding of the relevant elements in the external environment, the internal environment of the government, and the relevant stakeholders involved with each mission. These variables, which may span such issues as education, environment, technology, defense, and others, must then be put into context as part of a complex system. Using visioning tools and incorporating inputs from various agencies and nongovernment experts, the Center for Security Analysis and Assessment will map the range of possible interactions and outcomes across various time intervals, producing visions of possible future environments from the short term to the long term.

The center would provide policymakers with an ability to take stock of the status of both the internal system and the external environment, as well as to understand the decision points necessary to maintain the policymakers' objectives across the whole of the nation's systems.

By addressing all facets of national power as well as a full range of expertise to engage in short-, mid-, and long-term assessments of the global environment, the center will enable the country not only to react to the changing global environment but to preempt changes to that environment, and to play an active role in shaping the future.

Testing of Assumptions and Proposed Policies through Gaming, Systems Thinking, and Alternative Analysis.

Within the complex system that we inhabit, no arm of government creates or executes policy in a vacuum; policies can and do produce unanticipated and sometimes disproportional impacts in other areas. Moreover, the policy decisions that are made with a view to achieving short-term goals can produce unanticipated long-term effects.

The Center for Security Analysis and Assessment can serve as a place where policy options can be understood as part of a complex system and within an extended timeline. Proposed policies can be assessed to gauge potential implications, as well as tested against alternative options. As Robert Lempert argues, "Policymakers may not always welcome a critical spotlight on the potential weaknesses of their proposed strategies. But, if rigorous assessment of surprise becomes as commonplace as budgeting and accounting, policymakers will find it harder to ignore."[7]

One of the most critical functions of the center will be the capability for gaming issues of national importance. Gaming is usually considered the process of thinking through events in a step-by-step, point-counterpoint fashion to explore possible outcomes of certain courses of action compared to others. These processes enable thinking through situations that can occur before decisions are made through exercises of varying kinds. The processes should be developed to ensure a thorough investigation and analysis of the situation and exploration of positions on all sides of the question involved. These capabilities will range from "red teaming" proposed courses of action and developing step-by-step tabletop exercises meant to role play situations in foreign policy or peace negotiations, on one hand, to the development of alternative visions of the future and calculating risks associated with each one to determine which set of decisions should be made and which policies should be implemented to create the preferred future state, on the other hand.

Gaming has many forms including scenario-based planning. Gaming processes improve the ability to develop strategies and policies or choose specific decisions over others in a world of uncertainty. The objective of a game, however, is not to predict behaviors but to learn about the potential of certain behaviors and their effects on others and which sets of behaviors and therefore outcomes might be best for the "end game" one is looking for. Games are structured thinking processes that ultimately produce analysis and synthesis to improve decisionmaking regarding strategies and policies. They require holistic and systems thinking about specific issues.

The spectrum of games available in the Center will include traditional scenario-based "stories" associated with specific interagency issues or country teams, and "grand strategy" level issues such as "energy independence by 2050" or "sustainable peace in the Middle East."

The gaming capabilities within the Center will be available at many different levels of scale and complexity depending on the needs. Levels from "grand strategy" to tactical concerns are levels of scale. Levels of complexity can also be varied depending on the sets of issues to be examined. Levels of sophistication can also vary from the use of tabletop exercises that employ pencils and paper, to the use of algorithms in the development of software that can facilitate a variety of games using computer simulations.

Games can be developed at any level. The "grand strategy" level will be used to describe the highest level of strategy needed, usually at the global or country-to-country level. The "strategic" level suggests the whole agency or department or an institution such as the Army. The "operational" level suggests an organization such as a directorate or brigade. The "tactical" level can go as low as the individual in a group or a small group such as a platoon.

What is most important is that the mission of the exercise be identified so that clear objectives can be written and exercises developed to accomplish the mission. All games should have one thing in common. They should facilitate learning about a particular topic, course of action, or policy decision to better understand the dynamics of the environment surrounding the issue, the issue itself, the stakeholders, and players involved. Games are studies. In particular, decisions should be thought through looking holistically at the situation and determining the second, third, and fourth order effects of contemplated decisions. For example, tools as diverse as causal loop diagramming and mathematical techniques of operations research will be available in the Center and available for gaming as needed. Causal loop diagrams visually "map" the relationships between phenomena and decisions. Operations research techniques are frequently used to study costs and effectiveness of judgments. Many methods for strategy and policy analysis, synthesis, and systems thinking will be used. In fact, all suitable methods within the structured and disciplined processes that enable better thinking will be employed in the Center. According to Richard Kugler in his seminal work *Policy Analysis in National Security Affairs: New Methods for a New Era:*

> [The] U.S. Government will continue to face many difficult decisions in the national security arena because the future is hard to see, and the consequences of alternative policies are hard to predict . . . systems analysis can help improve the quality of these decisions . . . it can help the Government think clearly in times of uncertainty and during noisy debates about policy and strategy.[8]

Most of the games employed in the Center will be developed for the Center but will draw upon the myriad games that have been used over decades to think through "war" scenarios, but with the inclusion of other themes including economic, diplomatic, and environmental issues in addition to the traditional war-peace issues that games have played in the past. Learning through play is not only for children, but also is a major way for adults to prepare for the future; Games are for all who need to use imagination and knowledge, coupled with experimentation, to practice the way forward. As Arie De Gues says in *The Living Company: Habits for Survival in a Turbulent Business En-*

vironment, describing the original Royal Dutch Shell scenario process development:

> The decision-making process is in fact a learning process in any company and there are ways to improve the speed, if not the quality, of the decisions. The more in depth the simulation, and the more that "play" triggers the imagination and learning, the more effective the decision-making process seems to be.[9]

Conferences, Symposiums, and Public Engagement.

In addition to providing a context to inform the creation of policy, the center may also seek to contribute to public discourse on national security and educate policymakers at all levels of government on matters of the future. This may be accomplished through holding conferences and symposiums, issuing publications, and bringing together experts to assess the state of the world and the possible future environment.

APPLICATIONS

When the 44th President of the United States took office on January 20, 2009, he assumed responsibility for an overflowing portfolio of vexing challenges: two protracted wars, a deep recession, nuclear proliferation, global climate change, a ponderous and expensive healthcare system in desperate need of reform, and a failing education system, to name but a few. The challenges bearing down on Barack Obama were unprecedented in their number and complexity, and, one could argue, their pressing importance to the national's security and viability.

They were also unique for another reason: most, if not all, may have been avoided, mitigated, or reduced had previous administrations been endowed with greater foresight, had policymakers possessed an environment in which to test their assumptions, and had they been able to game potential impacts of their policies not only for the immediate future, but in the mid and long term.

What would the position of the United States in the world resemble today if, in 2003, policymakers demurred on invading Iraq on the basis of what we now understand to have been faulty intelligence? What of the state of the nation's coffers? Or of American soft power abroad? Looking further back, what might the world be like if, 50 years earlier, the Eisenhower administrated had engaged in a more rigorous assessment of the political climate in Iran before deciding to overthrow the Mosaddeq government? What if they had taken the time to challenge their assumptions regarding the strength of Iran's communist party, or had considered how a coup would impact American popularity in the region for decades to come? Would the 1979 revolution have occurred? Could the rise of a radical, politicized Islam have been stemmed? Would Iran now be threatening the balance of Middle Eastern power with a nuclear program?

Just as these challenges might have been mitigated or avoided if previous administrations had anticipated the short-, mid- and long-term impacts of policies, so too must the present administration craft policies that will target the diverse time frames. (See Figure 1-1.)

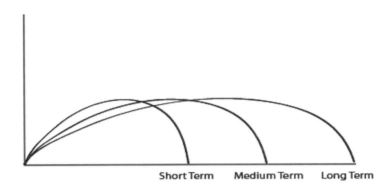

Figure 1-1. Diverse Policy Time Frames.

Consider the issue of climate change. Although not traditionally regarded as a national security issue, the prospect of increased world temperatures could significantly exacerbate security challenges facing the United States. Depending on the rate of warming, there exist a range of possible effects that we must begin preparing for—the worst of which may include mass population migrations, food and water shortages, ethnic conflicts, political instability, and military competition among great powers.

To inform policymakers of the multifarious issues raised by the prospect of global warming, the CSAA would engage in an assessment of a range of potential scenarios that could emerge across different time frames, including evaluating the likelihood and the potential ramifications of each. Some of the potential impacts of global warming across time are illustrated in Figure 1-2:

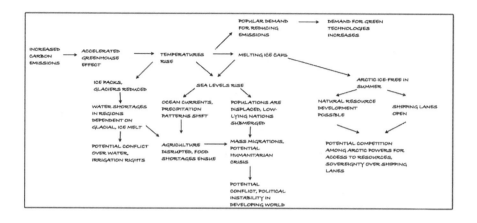

Figure 1-2. Possible Future Effects of Global Warming.

The scenarios shown in Figure 1-2 range from the immediate (melting glaciers, demand for green technologies), through the medium term (ice-free arctic in summer), to the long term (mass population displacements), and include developments that are both potentially advantageous and detrimental to the security of the United States.

Although debate continues over the extent to which global warming will alter the earth's systems, there is good reason nonetheless to pursue actions now that would greatly improve the nation's ability to cope with the effects of climate change—whatever they may be. Preemptive measures can and should begin now to curb CO_2 emissions, manage and prepare for the changing environment, exploit potential commercial opportunities, and mitigate the risk of humanitarian disasters and conflict. Without taking immediate action towards these ends, the United States may lose the opportunity to capitalize on the demand for green technologies and may forfeit the chance to find peaceful solutions to potential conflict. Such preventative

measures may include the following actions:
- Work towards the multilateral development of a legal framework governing use of Arctic shipping lanes.
- Invest in ice-breakers, train arctic mariners, improve patrol and emergency response capabilities in the Arctic.
- Engage in diplomatic dialogue among Arctic powers to resolve territorial resource issues before tensions have an opportunity to escalate.
- Develop and mine rare earth metals vital to many "green" technologies.
- Invest in research and development to gain a comparative advantage in green technologies.
- Encourage efficient personal, agricultural, and industrial water use, particularly in the American Southwest.
- Engage in capacity-building and develop the emergency response capabilities of states threatened by rising sea levels and internal displacement.
- Increase the U.S. military's ability to respond to humanitarian relief and disaster assistance operations.

In addition to providing policymakers with a context in which to evaluate priorities and pursue policy initiatives, the CSAA will also be capable of gaming the impacts of proposed policies and assessing the implications of new developments in the situation.

These insights, gleaned from the work of the CSAA, could mean the difference between poverty and abundance, innovation and stagnation, conflict and cooperation. The center, much like a GPS system, will not tell the country how to proceed, nor dictate what the ultimate destination must be. But it will at least serve to penetrate the fog of the future, and allow us to see what turns lie ahead.

ENDNOTES - CHAPTER 1

1. *Forging a New Shield,* Arlington, VA: Project on National Security Reform, 2008, p. 497.

2. Leon Fuerth, now a professor of international affairs and director of the Project on Forward Engagement, is a member of the Project on National Security Reform's guiding coalition and an advisor to the Vision Working Group.

3. Leon Fuerth, "Foresight and Anticipatory Governance," *Foresight,* Vol. 11, No. 4, 2009, p. 30.

4. Martha Crenshaw, "Terrorism, Strategies, and Grand Strategies," Russell D. Howard, Reid L. Sawyer, and Natasha E. Bajema, eds., *Terrorism and Counterterrorism: Understanding the New Security Environment, Readings and Interpretations,* 3rd Ed., New York: McGraw Hill, 2004.

5. Bruce Don, "What Can Complexity Teach Us about Policy," paper presented at RAND and the Woodrow Wilson Center for Scholars seminar series: *Decision Making in Complex Systems – Lessons for Public Policy,* Washington, DC, February 2002.

6. Yehezkel Dror, "Beyond Uncertainty: Facing the Inconceivable," *Technological Forecasting and Social Change,* Vol. 62, Nos. 1 and 2, 1999.

7. Robert Lempert, "Can Scenarios Help Policymakers Be Both Bold and Careful?" in Francis Fukuyama, ed., *Blindside: How to Anticipate Forcing Events and Wild Cards in Global Politics,* Baltimore, MD: Brookings Institution Press, 2007.

8. Richard Kugler, *Policy Analysis in National Security Affairs: New Methods for a New Era,* Washington, DC: National Defense University Press, 2006.

9. Arie De Gues, *The Living Company: Habits for Survival in a Turbulent Business Environment,* Boston, MA: Harvard Business Press, 2002.

CHAPTER 2

SCENARIO USE IN THE
PROJECT ON NATIONAL SECURITY REFORM

Sheila R. Ronis

INTRODUCTION

This chapter describes how scenarios were used in the development and testing of the Project on National Security Reform (PNSR) recommendations. Among the many techniques available, scenarios can be utilized in planning and execution, as well as in steady state and contingency contexts.

USES OF SCENARIOS

Since there are many different kinds of scenario-based processes used for different purposes, it is useful to consider scenario use in two overarching categories. The first category is the creation of "visions" in an aspirational context, answering the question "What do we want in the future?" The second category is used for stress testing proposed policies, strategies, plans, and courses of action. It is the category employed for the PNSR study, a process described in more detail later in this chapter.

Scenarios may be used primarily in these two different ways, but the processes of developing them can be very similar. Done correctly, scenario development involves techniques applied in a disciplined series of steps that generally come in the form of answering questions. The questions are simple in construction, but can demand thoughtful and often complex answers. The very notion of answering any question about a particular future is inherently challenging. Yet the essence of scenario use is about peering into an unknown and wrestling with what *might* be, absent the comfort of facts. The further one peers into the future, even sound assumptions can begin to seem unreliable. Over time, however, scenario-based processes have demonstrated their utility for multiple purposes and in numerous contexts.

THE PNSR SCENARIO DEVELOPMENT METHODOLOGY

The PNSR scenario process can be summed up in seven steps: (1) Determine the purpose and scope (in years and breadth of actors or system components to be visualized) of the exercise; (2) Development of a questionnaire to be given to experts; (3) Development of a list of experts across many fields; (4) Invitation to experts to develop timelines into the future; (5) Aggregation, analysis, and synthesis of data to develop scenarios; (6) Stress testing the scenarios; and (7) Stress testing a particular course of action within the scenarios or developing a new vision. Let us describe each of the seven in detail.[1]

1. **Determine the purpose and scope of the exercise** (in years and breadth of actors or system components to be visualized, number of scenarios to use, and iterative time blocks to be studied along the way). In this step, one might begin by stating that there is a need to look out 25 years (or more or less) into the future regarding the state of affairs for the Department of X. The purpose, then, of the exercise would be to determine how all the system components, whatever they might be in 25 years, could be operating success-

fully in a particular or in multiple contexts. The scope might be stated in terms of how many component parts of the Department of X should be visualized—perhaps the vision would only be for a sub-system of a large departmental system that is in question. The scope might also be stated in terms of how many different scenarios one might wish to use to develop a composite view of the environmental factors in 25 years. Finally, the scope may be described in terms of how many time iterations over the next 25 years the exercise will examine. For example, it may wish to examine the leading decades preceding the 25-year end state—the 10-year mark, the 20-year mark, and then the 25-year mark. Once these pieces are in place, a statement of purpose and scope is developed to guide the remaining steps.

2. **Development of a questionnaire**. As noted earlier, this next step becomes the hub of the visioning process. The right questions will guide all the other steps and will act as the keel upon which all the scenario details will be built. These questions might include: What is going on in the world that the system needs to know about today and into the different futures—10, 20, 25 years? How does the system work today? How will the system change over these time blocks? What does the system need to know today to be successful? What will the system need to know in the future to be successful? What does the system need to do starting today to improve the probability that the system can shape the future that it wants? All of these are put into a questionnaire that will be used to canvass the very best minds in the appropriate fields pertaining to these future environments. Their answers will eventually populate a database that when spread visually over the course of a linear 25-year calendar is the beginning of what can be called "a future history."

3. **Development of a list of experts across many fields.** Perhaps the most counterintuitive step in the entire visioning process is in this step of gathering of experts "in appropriate fields." What may be counterintuitive is the fact that all experts may be relevant when it comes to scenario development. As an inherently systems theory-based process, it is recognized that even the most odd or tangential fields can have dramatic second and third order effects on any primary environmental area of interest. Music, for example, may have as many global political and cultural ramifications as religion. Or the reduced scores of American children in math and science in relation to children around the world may have connections to the industrial and economic competitiveness of the United States. The question then becomes how to appropriately limit this scope to what is manageable in the exercise while casting as wide a net as possible.

4. **Experts are invited to develop timelines into the future.** This is the part of the exercise where real creativity is used most and there are few limits. The term "Timelines into the future" is synonymous with "future histories." Both are simply timelines looked at from one of two perspectives: from now forward to 25 years, or from 25 years looking backwards to now. In either case, the process is essentially the same although the two perspectives can make for some interesting nuances in creativity. The steps here are to conduct individual interviews with each expert in a different field in a room with post-it notes and a long piece of paper taped to a wall or electronically if possible. The expert is given a pen and told to post ideas about his/her field along the timeline with an emphasis in our example on the three sub time blocks of 10, 20 and 25 years. Once that is achieved, the expert is asked to fill

in the blank spots as much as possible with ideas or innovations upon which each of his future ideas would depend. For example, if the expert put down, "in 20 years from now, we will have flying cars," he/she might then put down a note, "in 10 years we will have the technology to create really small and light car engines with the same power as today." These interdependent links are critical to creating a more seamless narrative of that expert's field between now and 25 years. The sum total of this work would then become either a future history or a timeline to the future depending on your preferred perspective. The sum total of over 100 different expert timelines culminates in a rich mosaic of ideas. In the case of PNSR, 133 timelines were developed.

5. **The aggregation, analysis, and synthesis of data to develop scenarios.** The 100 expert timelines when populated in a database become a composite scenario of the future in these various fields. Once the data is organized, trends usually appear. Notes are taken, and the scenarios are then developed based on the trends emerging from the database. Once developed, the scenarios are sent out to experts for review.

6. **Stress testing the scenarios.** The review process becomes a test drive of the scenario. Each one of the experts studies and then comments on the trend analyses and the scenario plausibility. Once all is consolidated, the scenario is ready for use by other customers.

7. **Stress testing a particular course of action or creating a new system vision.** Once the scenario is ready, it can be used in either of the two categories discussed earlier. In the case of creating a vision, an organization's leadership would conduct a series of facilitated workshops based on scenario immersion by

all the members of that group. In our example, the upper tier of Department X management might seclude themselves in a room for several hours a day over the course of 2 days role-playing in this hypothesized world of the future scenario. The facilitated discussions would allow for a step-by-step process of discovery in how that future world might affect Department X and, better yet, how Department X can best position itself in process, structure, people, etc., to be most successful in that future. Finally, Department X can begin to consider steps as part of a future plan to build organizational improvements over the course of the next several years aiming towards a new vision of itself emanating from this experience.

In the category of stress testing a course of action, the same process may be used, but instead of a blank sheet of paper and a wide open discovery process of how the future could unfold, the participants game their already proposed course of action of policy and/or strategy against the different futures. In this process, the facilitator may spend a bit more time conducting and then recording a more typical sequence of action, reaction, counter-reaction of one part of a course of action against several parts of a given future in various areas of interest. For example, the group may say that Department X will prepare to render a particular service in 5 years and provide it to all developing world countries. The reaction to that by the facilitator now role playing or red teaming (red teaming is the use of an experimental "red" team to silently compete with an established team in performance of identical tasks, and then compare results), would be that this service causes an unfortunate secondary reaction eliminating local cottage industries, causing violence and unrest to spread. The counterreaction might then be to not flood the market with the service but to build the industries in those countries so that they can actually create jobs. The problem is wrestled with from all angles using scenario-based stress testing.

Because few organizations or governments actually go through such steps to search for the answers to these deeper questions, their ability to accomplish any objectives in the long term and often even in the near term becomes significantly degraded in the myopias of the immediate. Scenario use transforms minds and hearts, and leads others to practical actions towards concrete aims.

It is important to remember that there is an infinite number of potential futures, so that a scenario of the future is not a forecast or a prediction but a planning tool to think about events that could happen in the future—before they occur. As long as the scenario is plausible and properly developed, stress testing proposed courses of action leads to new insights and new knowledge and can be very helpful in making decisions.

Scenarios are one type of "vision" of the future. Another one is the rather popularized "vision" statement for a company or organization such as the grandiose goals appearing in an organization's annual report that talks about what its members want their organization to become over the next several years – e.g., "the leader in transportation products and services," - to borrow an example from General Motors. These statements can be used to help communicate where the organization is going and build consensus with key stakeholders, employees, suppliers, unions, constituents, stockholders, and so on. The visioning process is especially useful for large complex organizations where multiple systems must come together to create the ultimate product or service for the customer. The process of visioning is sometimes more important than the vision itself and enables side-by-side learning of employees and senior leadership together, as a team. Yet, too often these visions are created by public relations firms or planning staffs without the benefit of the actual process itself.

SCENARIO USE IN PNSR

The process described above was used by PNSR to develop scenarios and stress test the major project findings and recommendations of *Forging a New Shield*. While stress testing the recommendations, it became clear that each one improved the current system significantly, some more, some less. (See Appendix A.)

Determine the Purpose and Scope of the Exercise.

The process began by enlisting the assistance of experts in many fields including a cross-section of the sciences and engineering. On behalf of Lieutenant General Brent Scowcroft and Dr. John Hennessy, the co-chairs of the Committee on Scientific Communication and National Security (CSCANS), Dr. Patricia Wrightson, Director of the Committee on Scientific Communication and National Security at the National Academies, invited a select group of scientists to participate in a day-long workshop on the future of science and security, co-sponsored by CSCANS and PNSR. On April 9, 2008, the scientists participated in a meeting at the National Academies in which the future was further explored. Facilitated by Jim Burke, the director of the TASC Futures Group, the scientists explored issues of the past and present, but particularly the future.

CSCANS, a standing committee of the National Research Council, worked with the Vision Working Group (VWG) of PNSR to address how scientists understand and assess the future. The two groups co-hosted the joint futures and forecasting workshop on the Future of Science and Security. The agenda included lively dialogue, including discussion of ways to solicit scientists' and other experts' views of emerging trends and future events that could affect national security.

This series of events helped the VWG develop the purpose and the scope of the eventual scenario development to include what questions should be included in the questionnaire.

Development of a Questionnaire.

Following these events, the VWG, working with colleagues from the TASC Futures Group, determined the best approach for a survey instrument in which individuals from many fields would participate in an online questionnaire. Based on previous feedback from the National Academies workshop and the TASC Futures Group, a questionnaire was finalized that would be used to populate a data set depicting different events through the eyes of multiple experts across a 50-year timeline into the future.

Development of a list of experts across many fields. Following the development of the questionnaire, the VWG created a list of leading national experts in many disciplines across the sciences, engineering, futurists, and other fields too numerous to list here.

Experts are invited to develop timelines into the future. The questionnaire was sent to about 1,500 experts by email. The goal set was for a 2-3 percent return — enough to claim a valid sampling. The VWG actually obtained a 9 percent (133) response rate.

The aggregation, analysis, and synthesis of data to develop scenarios. The experts' insights on future trends and milestones were aggregated, analyzed, and synthesized to build a composite future scenario and to develop trend analyses. The trends identified by the experts were then woven into the nine scenarios representing the three time horizons; 2020, 2040, and 2060.

Stress testing the scenarios. Before the scenarios could be used to stress test the recommendations of the Project, the VWG asked the Commandants of three schools at the National Defense University to choose selected faculty who teach in the national security curriculum of each school to review all nine scenarios and provide feedback regarding their validity. This faculty included those from: (1) The National War College; (2) The Industrial College of the Armed Forces; and (3) The Joint Forces Staff College. Based on the feedback of these faculty members many changes were made to the scenarios.

Stress Testing the Major PNSR Solution Sets. Finally, the VWG used the nine scenarios to stress test the major recommendations of the PNSR over the course of three sessions, using all of the chief concept developers for the project study (including those in structure, human capital, knowledge management, congressional services, and process). The scenarios were intentionally designed to stress the concept developers' study recommendations from several angles: (1) What did they think were the key stressors in the scenario from their sub-system perspective such as human capital reforms? (2) How well was their sub-system able to anticipate the scenario problems? (3) If unable to prevent/remove the threat, how well was their sub-system able to react? (4) How well was their sub-system able to recover? and (5) How well does the overall national security system proposed by the PNSR function as a whole in these scenarios?

The letter below was given to the PNSR concept developers (the PNSR Working Group Leaders) to start the process.

> Dear PNSR Working Group Chairs and Members:
>
> The Vision Working Group has developed the following alternative future national security scenarios for your consideration. These brief scenarios are designed to provide a range of perspectives on how the next few decades might unfold. The purpose of these scenarios is to assist you in the hard work of creating PNSR policy recommendations that will stand the test of time.
>
> The National Security Act of 1947 has survived largely intact for 60 years, despite major social, technological, economic, environmental, and political changes. These cumulative changes are a primary reason why the Project on National Security Reform is necessary.
>
> Similarly, we will face extraordinary changes in the next 60 years. In fact, many futurists, forecasters, and technologists believe that the rate of change in the next decades will be faster than the decades preceding.
>
> It is with this in mind that we were asked to create a set of scenarios that would provoke discussion and debate within your working groups and hopefully lead to better, more resilient policy recommendations.
>
> As a caveat, these scenarios have been intentionally designed to stress your recommendations from sev-

eral angles. The scenarios should not be viewed as predictions of a probable future, but rather glimpses into plausible alternative futures. The scenarios are intentionally inconsistent and oft times bleak, all in the interest of provoking a wider range of conversation.

Each scenario is followed by specific discussion questions to ponder. Some questions may be more applicable to your working group than others. Here are some general questions you can use when reading each scenario: 1) how would my working group's recommendations function in the scenario presented? 2) are there problems or solutions identified here that we have not addressed? 3) if this future is not desirable, what choices should we be making today to avoid it?

In an effort to make the scenarios more accessible and tangible, we have generally used the actual names of countries and locations. Other names could easily be substituted for the ones used.

Last, but not least, I would like to thank the National Academies for their help in eliciting the future insights of dozens of leading scientists and engineers for this effort. In addition, we received insights from forward-thinking contributors in other fields too numerous to mention, as well as review comments from the Industrial College of the Armed Forces, the National War College, the Joint Forces Staff College and Argonne National Laboratory. I hope you find these scenarios interesting and useful.

Sincerely,

Dr. Sheila R. Ronis, Chair
PNSR Vision Working Group

Throughout all the steps, the VWG benefited from the expert assistance of the TASC Futures Group led by Jim Burke and Christopher Waychoff with Matthew Russell and John Meagher in the development of the Pre-Reform scenarios. The final Post-Reform Alternative National Security Scenarios (2020-60) were developed by Christopher Waychoff. Dr. Sheila Ronis, the Chair of the VWG, and Jim Burke, Northrop Grumman's Senior Futurist, facilitated the discussions with the PNSR concept developers. As the PNSR concept developers worked through the scenarios, it became clear that each of the PNSR recommended solutions performed differently in the different scenario situations. Strengths and weaknesses of the solution sets gradually emerged, leading to eventual adjustments to PNSR recommendations before publication.

THE PRE- AND POST-REFORM SCENARIOS

The PNSR concept developers were presented first with scenarios during the initial process of developing recommendations. These scenarios were called the Pre-Reform Scenarios published in Chapter 2. Later, the VWG updated these same scenarios based upon the final PNSR recommendations. In other words, several selected final recommendations were actually written into the scenarios to see how they would stand in the future. These final scenarios were called Post-Reform scenarios. The Post-Reform scenarios were developed by asking: "Would this have happened in the same way had these PNSR recommendations been in place starting in 2009?" These updated Post-Reform scenarios focused on the major impacts of the PNSR recommendations on the scenarios. They are published in Chapter 3.

As with any use of scenarios, they are intended only to be suggestive and not definitive. They do not represent a complete narrative of every system impact in any future though the nine simply gave the Project leadership a glimpse into a plausible reaction to the PNSR recommendations.

ENDNOTES - CHAPTER 2

1. The methodology used in the development of the PNSR scenarios is based upon the work by Sheila Ronis, *Timelines into the Future: Strategic Visioning Methodology for Government, Business and Other Organizations*, Mansfield, TX: Hamilton Press, 2007.

CHAPTER 3

THE PRE-REFORM NINE SCENARIOS

Chris Waychoff
Matthew Russell
John Meagher
Jim Burke

2020
Scenario 1: Red Death
Scenario 2: People's War
Scenario 3: A Grand Strategy

2040
Scenario 4: A New Economy
Scenario 5: Pax Robotica
Scenario 6: Who Holds the High Ground
Scenario 7: A Brave New World

2060
Scenario 8: A Warm Reception
Scenario 9: It's a Small World

2020

Scenario 1: Red Death.

In this scenario, we meet a country struggling to get back on its feet after a major biological attack and witness a debate about the future role of the U.S. Government both at home and abroad.

Dr. Meishan Prosper, MD, ScD, cycled through the various web feeds of the inaugural Strength Through Unity Summit looking for anyone she knew. She assumed it would be unlikely, given the death toll over the last 3 years. The first response and medical communities had been the hardest hit, but no group of Americans had gone untouched.

The word that was usually used was "decimated," but she knew that decimated literally meant the death of 1 in 10 people. The Red Death, attacking the victims' central nervous systems, had taken one quarter of the world's population seemingly overnight and left an additional quarter paralyzed, with few people to care for them.

It had struck with no warning. It had not been picked up directly by any of the urban or airport biosensors put in place over a decade ago when the United States had feared an imminent biological attack following September 11, 2001 (9/11). After bin Laden had been found dead in a tribal village in Pakistan, the desire to improve the biosensors' capabilities had waned, and other priorities had risen to the top.

Of course, the sensors of those days would not have picked up the bio threats of 2017. Biological research had made massive strides in the intervening decade and a half. Genetics, proteomics, and synthetic biology had all surged forward with the increasing automation and miniaturization of biological research.

By 2017, biological research had become much more the domain of information hackers than of beakers and glass vials. Following an exponential rate of change, the capability to manufacture and modify biological agents had long since become cheap and easy to acquire despite international prohibitions. The attack could have come from anywhere.

Even if most of the survivors had not been told to stay in their homes, there were not enough people to maintain transportation, distribution, and public order. There were not enough skilled workers to run farms, factories, or public water and sanitation systems. Trade ceased. Foreign oil supplies ran out. Power plants and generators went silent. For all intents and purposes, the world had stopped. People looked inward, and national governments gradually dissolved. The global, national, and local economies collapsed, causing widespread starvation, disease, and violence. The situation was desperate and hopeless.

The United States had fractured along state and then local lines. Some communities, closer to their rural roots and managing their own security, began to show signs of recovery as soon as the virus had burned itself out a year ago. Larger, more urban areas had been mostly deserted as food stocks ran out and only now were showing signs of life.

Today, the U.S. Government was making its first tentative efforts to reestablish centralized national governance. Some parts of the country were eager to return to the way life had been before the Red Death. Other parts were leery of their neighbors and thought that the Red Death was proof that a centralized government was not the answer. Some pockets of Americans had declared their independence and were preparing to defend themselves against all comers.

This pattern was replicated around the world. New political boundaries were being established. Many national borders, drawn 100 years earlier by departing colonialists, were now being redrawn by local tribes and ethnic groups. In most places, the populations were too exhausted to fight over this new political reality, but in other regions, warlords, demagogues, and nationalist leaders seized the opportunity to engage in horrific acts of ethnic cleansing.

A vocal minority at the Summit argued vehemently for the need to reestablish a strong Federal Government to face this new world. They feared that U.S.

leadership of the world over the previous 80 years would be supplanted by whichever major power could recover first. Dr. Prosper allowed herself a brief smile over this "recovery gap."

Dr. Prosper, representing the Empire State of Georgia, could be counted among the remaining representatives to the Summit who were varying shades of "isolationist." They wanted no part of the wider world, except perhaps for trade on the strictest of terms.

Dr. Prosper knew this attitude did not come from the objective, scientific part of her brain, but rather from seeing her family, friends, and colleagues die around her. She did not want to risk that ever happening again.

Dr. Prosper had been at her office at the Centers for Disease Control (CDC) in Atlanta, Georgia, when the first hints of a major pandemic had been picked up through syndromic surveillance systems, first in Washington, DC, and then from all the capitals of the world.

She spent the next 2 months dividing her time between the CDC's Biosafety Level 4 lab and its telepresence media center before the remnants of her team and the Army team at Fort Detrick, Maryland, determined that the pathogen was artificial and had been released at what turned out to be the last meeting of the United Nations (UN) General Assembly.

Occurring just before a scheduled recess, dozens of infected diplomats had returned to their capitals to report on their activities to department executives. These executives, in turn, briefed their heads of government, and within 2 weeks time, the world's governments were largely decimated.

With the U.S. Government reeling, the state governments acted with varying degrees of effectiveness to the profound threat. Some states had inadequate or poorly resourced plans and succumbed immediately. Others were able to maintain ring quarantines and sanctuaries for a time, but with individuals evading checkpoints to find loved ones, the Red Death eventually came to every corner of the country.

Dr. Prosper shifted in her seat to listen more closely to the representative of the Free State of the Rockies. She could tell by his full mission oriented protective posture (MOPP) gear — gas mask and full body suit — that the Free State was not going to swallow a new national government easily. Its people were skeptical that a newly formed Federal Government would do what it needed to to keep them safe. Many Free Staters had died from untested vaccines the Federal Government had rushed to many parts of the country. Now, they were unconvinced by any federal assurances.

Despite, or perhaps because of, the fact that she had designed both the unsuccessful and eventually successful vaccines, Dr. Prosper understood their concerns. After all, the world was full of people with the means and motivation to attack again, and the original perpetrators of the Red Death had never been found.

Discussion.

- How can the United States plan and prepare for a catastrophe so devastating that it would shatter national governments worldwide?
- Is the U.S. leadership adequately protected?
- How resilient should continuity of government plans be? Should they extend beyond the Federal Government?

- How do you balance the roles of the federal, state, and local governments during a catastrophic disaster? Government and industry?
- How do you maintain the medical infrastructure when you have millions of incapacitated patients?
- How long would it take the world to recover from this catastrophe and which countries will end up on top? What will happen to the world if the United States loses its leading status?
- Do biological defense strategies anticipate emerging bio agent design and production capabilities?
- How do you gain and maintain political support for investment programs when the threat is either novel or not viewed as urgent?

Scenario 2: People's War.

In this scenario, the United States faces global asymmetric warfare against a nuclear-armed great power. The entire Federal Government is caught in the conundrum of how to respond to anonymous attacks at home and abroad while avoiding an escalation to nuclear war.

Intelligence Specialist Robert Wong slammed his hand down on his desk. The meeting in the Director's office had not gone as planned. For the past 3 weeks, he had raised red flags only to be shot down by his more senior peers. He was being rash. He did not understand the bigger picture. It was a local police matter. He did not have evidence. And now they were looking at him suspiciously!

Well, what evidence did you need when key U.S. Government personnel were being selectively assassinated by Chinese nationals? Just because the Chinese government claimed the assassins were grad students acting on their own patriotic initiative did not mean we should believe them.

At least this time he had arm-wrestled a footnote with his dissenting opinion into the latest estimate. Why couldn't they see it? Just because the attacks were not being carried out by soldiers in uniform, it did not take a genius to figure out that China was fighting a conventional war by other means.

The war had begun 5 weeks ago, just as the new nationalist Taiwanese President was to declare his nation's independence. Before he could make his address, the power went off across Taiwan, and defense radars went down. The U.S. Pacific Fleet, which had been sent into the Taiwan Straits before the speech as a show of support, were driven back out of strike range by a sudden and overwhelming barrage of intelligent, supersonic cruise missiles from the land, sea, and air. The missiles had saturated the U.S. fleet's air defenses, exhausted its defensive batteries, and sunk a number of ships before the fleet could stage a tactical withdrawal. This left the Taiwanese government to fight street by street with embedded sleeper agents and Chinese special forces paratroopers.

The U.S. President, hoping to avoid a larger and possibly nuclear war, disallowed long-range counterstrikes by the U.S. fleet and Air Force in the hopes that a negotiated settlement could be reached. China, claiming a misunderstanding, readily agreed to talks, while fighting continued on Taiwan.

Two weeks later, Wong started to see patterns of a wider covert war in sporadic events occurring on U.S. soil and with U.S. interests abroad. The increasing murders were the first clue. Key intelligence and military officials, leading doctors and engineers, and operations managers of critical manufacturing plants were killed according to some indecipherable plan.

Next came seemingly random power outages and overloads and the shutdown of public safety, aviation, and industrial systems. Anonymous commands from hackers around the world had been sent through secret backdoors embedded in computer chips years ago. Businesses and government agencies that had consolidated their information systems around a single, dominant operating system were shut down by a torrent of viruses, worms, and Trojan horses.

It was obvious to Wong that China was playing hardball to get the United States to acquiesce to its "reunification" of China, reduce U.S. influence in Asia, and accept China's full parity on the world stage. Around the world, Chinese allies and partners were halting mineral and gas shipments to the United States and its allies in Europe and Japan. Global industrial supply chains were being shut down at the lowest tiers, halting production of numerous U.S. weapon systems and other critical items. Chinese ships had "accidentally" broken down in the Panama Canal, and Panama was making no effort to clear the way. Piracy in the shipping lanes had spiked. Maoist guerillas had started new offensives in several countries in South America, Africa, and Asia.

It was clear to Wong that China was flexing newfound muscles and was going to squeeze the United States both at home and abroad until it achieved its ends. When would the country wake up and do something?

Discussion.

- How do you approach an asymmetrical war fought abroad or on U.S. soil with a major nuclear power?
- At what point do economic and cyber attacks become grounds for a larger conventional or nuclear war?
- How do you safeguard your international supply chains when the world is increasingly interdependent and the lowest tiers are all but invisible?
- In government discussions, how do you balance the need for consensus and the need to hear all voices?
- How are the roles of the military, law enforcement, and intelligence coordinated?
- How do you protect your critical infrastructure and key personnel from sleeper agents on U.S. soil?
- How do you balance human rights and security when dealing with a potentially hostile subgroup within the émigré community?
- Could the United States acquiesce to Chinese demands in such a situation and maintain its credibility?

Scenario 3: A Grand Strategy.

In this scenario, we explore the utility of an integrated grand strategy development capability for smoothing the transition from one presidential administration to another.

President-elect Anne Cummings stepped down into the well of the large conference room with her entourage. The lush blue carpet and warm wooden panels created a hushed effect, almost like entering an old library or church. A bird fluttered across the oval skylight. "Was that real sky?" she wondered.

Tom Hughes, the Director of the National Strategy Integration and Visioning Agency, strode across the carpet and extended his hand. "Welcome back, Governor. We are honored to have you here today."

"It is my pleasure, Tom. It's good to see you again in person. It's been a couple years since we held the Governors Convention here," she said with a warm smile. "You know Dr. Tyrone Chandra, my National Security Advisor; Ms. Catalina Sharp, my economic advisor; and Ms. Akemi Takahashi, my long-range planner?"

"Yes, good to see you all again. Akemi has been working very closely with us and her predecessor to refine the underlying model assumptions. I'm happy to say that not much tweaking was necessary. We paid pretty close attention to the campaign," beamed the Director.

"I'd also like to welcome the folks conferencing in," the Director said, indicating the faces strung out along the top edge of the screen that wrapped floor-to-ceiling 270 degrees around the conference room. "We are pleased to have your transition liaisons join us from the various department strategy offices, along with senior representatives of the outgoing Simpson administration. Welcome all."

"My mission today is to acquaint you with the general operation of the National Strategy Integration and Visioning Agency and its departmental satellite offices," announced the Director.

"NSIVA was created in 2013 to assist the President and his administration in developing a dynamic national grand strategy. The ability to create such a strategy was complicated by interagency stovepipes and rice bowls, political constraints on free and open discussion, and the technical difficultly of developing an integrated strategy in an increasingly complicated and interconnected world.

"The hope for the new organization was that it would not only be a safe place to debate, develop, test, and monitor long-range strategies, but that it could be an objective source of information that could withstand a change in administration. The problem, of course, was that pure objectivity was a mirage. Despite the best intentions and the selection of generally open-minded staff, bias and ideology always crept back in.

"The answer was to embrace varying points of view . . . to model and evaluate all points of view, rather than trying to find the one correct view, . . ." continued the Director. "As I hope Akemi has told you, our bipartisan, or rather multi-partisan, process is now ensured through our agency's host of checks and balances. These measures touch on all our activities ranging from how we hire and rotate our staff to how we build our models and debate the results.

"We also found that an open process keeps us honest, so we have developed an extensive outreach process to participants across the political spectrum, in government, industry, and academia. Our public discussion boards are particularly lively — there is nothing some posters like better than catching us with an unsupported assumption or an incorrect application of an algorithm," chuckled the Director.

"So are all points of view deemed to be of equal value and effectiveness?" asked Dr. Chandra, the incoming national security advisor.

"I wouldn't put it that way. While all points of view are captured and modeled, their value and effectiveness are determined by many other factors within the modeling system. Positions must be supported by evidence or coherent logic paths. If they are simply assertions, they will be flagged as such," replied the Director. "Why don't we look at an example?"

Swiping the screen of his wristwatch, the Director brought the main wall to animated life as a timeline stretched from 1980 at one end to 2080 at the other.

"Let's run a quick 'what if' scenario," said the Director as he walked to a large, inclined touchscreen table in the center of the room. Waving his hand over a world map, he highlighted the countries of the nascent Latin American Union. The main wall glowed with event and trend markers in a rainbow of colors.

"This view here is as close to a normative, objective view as we can produce. As you see, it's pretty sparse and contains only elements that are demonstrable, accepted facts or trends that have been broadly agreed upon within the statistical boundaries indicated."

"If we call up your administration's view," the Director said as he subvocalized a command to the wall, "we see there is much more detail at this level. We can also cycle through the department views…notice the intersections where one department's strategy runs into another department's."

"What are the flashing icons?" asked Dr. Chandra.

"The flashing icons represent new elements that have been placed on the wall by the system's estimation engine, but have not yet been validated by our team members. This one here is an analysis by the State Department's Latin America Desk of General Secretary Chávez's recent address to the LAU General Assembly. As you can see, if I tap on the icon there is a complete argument map supporting the analysis, plus a video of the speech."

"Do you get a feed of all operational and intelligence information?" quizzed Dr. Chandra.

"No, we don't. We are neither an operations center, nor an intelligence fusion center. We are strictly an open source, meta-analysis center, integrating the best analysis of our government and public partners. We find that what we lose in not having access to the latest classified information is more than compensated for by our ability to have an open dialogue with a wide variety of experts and stakeholders. Moreover, our timeline is a little longer. We are not overwhelmed by the day's in-basket. We have the luxury, as well as the responsibility, to look longer term."

"Can we look at the trends from an economic point of view?" queried the President-elect's economic advisor.

"Certainly. Here are the administration's economic trend lines under the 'what if' assumption that Mexico joins the LAU embargo of oil to the United States."

"What is that red line receding into the background?" she asked.

"That indicates a strong sensitivity between this economic scenario and domestic politics in the U.S. Southwest," the Director replied.

"Have you gotten to the point where the grand strategy writes itself?" joked the President-Elect.

"Hah, hah, no, no, the primary job of the models, analysis, and visualizations you have seen is to get our collective thinking organized. There are too many options, too many impacts, too many interrelationships for the human mind to follow without assistance.

"The Agency helps avoid continually reinventing the wheel and arguing past one another. The real work, the work of finding common ground, crafting solutions, and implementing these solutions to achieve national objectives only begins here with your people, aided by our staff. Decisionmaking remains the domain of the President and Congress."

Discussion.

- How important is having a dynamic national grand strategy?
- What is the relationship among national security strategy, economic strategy, diplomatic strategy, public health strategy, etc.?
- How can the strategies of the federal agencies be integrated better? The strategies of the executive branch and Congress? States? Industry?
- What can be done to smooth the transition between administrations?
- How can knowledge developed during one administration be shared with another?
- Is it possible to have open, honest, rational political debate within the government?
- Should the public be invited to take part in strategy development?
- Can technology be used to extend the understanding and thinking of policymakers?
- Can the United States look beyond 2-year and 4-year political cycles?

2040

Scenario 4: A New Economy.

In this scenario, the United States faces its worst economic crisis since the Great Depression. The crisis is a perfect storm of the unintended consequences of new technologies, policies, court decisions, and popular expectations.

Ron Guilder craned his neck to get a better view of the podium on the stage in front of the Washington Monument. He could have gotten a better view if he had stayed home and jacked into his home virtuality system.

"What do we want?" challenged the speaker.

"JOBS!" responded the sea of angry faces.

"When do we want them?"

"NOW!"

Guilder always felt a little awkward chanting and did not join in. It seemed so proletarian to him. He had been, after all, the Chief Financial Officer of a Fortune 500 company and did not consider himself working class.

"1, 2, 3, 4, WE WANT LIFE AS BEFORE," the speaker and crowd chanted in unison. "5, 6, 7, 8, GIVE US JOBS OR MEET YOUR FATE."

Guilder was not alone in the crowd. Many of the protestors in fact were former white collar workers who had been displaced years ago by the ever increasing acumen of enterprise management systems. In this crowd and concurrently around the country, former managers intermingled with blue collar labor and service workers, all eased out of their jobs by smart machines and smarter software.

At first, Guilder had embraced his new life of early retirement and leisure. He had known for a while that automated management systems could do a better, faster job of financial planning than he could. Robotic manufacturing and intelligent management systems had streamlined business, lowering prices on goods and services to the point where everyone had the basics plus many luxuries too. A monthly government stipend was all that was necessary to live the good life.

Of course, it had not been like that in the late 1920s and early 1930s when intelligent machines first started to displace workers in droves. Unlike the gradual disappearance of telephone switchboard operators and secretarial pools in the 20th century, the rapid displacement of blue collar and service workers left a large portion of the population suddenly without jobs and no hope for future employment. Food riots, martial law, tent cities, work relief programs, robot sabotage, and union busting became a sign of the times.

The Income Preservation Act of 2034 was Congress's first attempt to stabilize the situation. Businesses were required to maintain a specific percentage of workers, whether there was work for them to do or not, and provide mandatory pensions for the rest. In addition, annual stipends were disbursed from the Treasury to unemployed individuals. The newly repurposed Department of Labor and Leisure actively promoted the benefits of a leisure society to ease the transition from the standard 3-day work week to not working at all. Most people could not have been happier: unlimited free time, cheap goods and services, and fully immersive virtual entertainment.

To pay for this government largess, taxes were raised on businesses, and those few individuals who still had jobs (designers, innovators, entertainers, athletes), owned or operated businesses, or lived off family wealth. The combined federal and state tax rates soared over 90 percent as the government strove to pay for escalating stipends to keep the public happily at home. The tax increases, the restricted labor market, and the looming threat of industrial nationalization had the effect of closing some businesses and compelling others to flee to tax havens overseas. Businesses raised prices in an attempt to keep up with the rapidly changing tax structure. As the tax base dried up, the President pressured a weak Federal Reserve to increase the money supply. Slowly but surely, inflation rose.

Over time, the previously mollified public began to feel the pinch. Stipends were not keeping up with prices. In 2039, an appeal to the U.S. Supreme Court discovered a Right to Food and Shelter in the penumbra of a living Constitution. The government began to print more money to meet these new entitlements. Last month, the automated investment management systems around the world monitoring this latest dilution of the value of U.S. currency began to dump dollars onto the world market. The U.S. stock markets crashed. U.S. Treasury securities, municipal bonds, and corporate bonds all dropped to their lowest possible ratings. Businesses closed, trade ceased, world markets collapsed—a vicious cycle of hyperinflation took hold pushing 100,000 percent.

Guilder seethed with unfocused anger. A loaf of 14-grain artisan rye bread now cost him $2 million dollars. Somebody needed to do something! But what? As a former CFO, he understood the economics, he understood the trap the country had fallen into. He himself had enjoyed the benefits of the new economy. Now this! He could not feed his family. His life savings were gone. Where could he find hope?

In the distance, he saw black smoke rising from the burning effigy of the President. A young Silverite thug, looking for a fight, shoved past him toward the acrid smoke. A surveillance drone hummed overhead.

Discussion.

- What is the role of national economic health in national security?
- How would a world with large-scale unemployment affect national security?
- How would a major financial crisis affect our position in the world?
- Can the U.S. political system survive without a middle class?
- What is the role of the military in a national uprising?
- What interagency mechanisms are affected by long-term changes in workforce composition and structure? In unions?
- Given the shutdown of the nation's economy, how would federal, state, and local governments handle a nationwide emergency relief effort? How would state and local governments fund their own activities?
- How would we coordinate with international organizations and foreign countries offering aid?
- Would we restrict emigration of people from the United States? The rich? The poor? The educated? The innovative? Businesses?
- Will surveillance systems reduce the likelihood of violent uprisings?

Scenario 5: Pax Robotica.

In this scenario, we explore the intersection of unmanned robotic warfare and on-the-ground diplomacy. This scenario depends upon the continuation of current accelerating trends in robotics and sensors technology, as well as a public policy choice to enable greater real-time interaction between the military, diplomatic, and intelligence arms of the U.S. Government.

Total dominance of the battlefield had been achieved in just 3 days. From command bunkers in Colorado, override controllers watched as autonomous robotic swarms annihilated the loyalist Homeland Guard with minimal collateral damage. The remainder of the Chuntu Army saw what was coming, listened to the broadcast warnings, dropped their weapons, and ran home as fast as they could. The genocidal Chuntu leadership was captured or killed in brief, but brutal, house-to-house fighting with wheeled, crawling, and airborne robots.

Now, 2 weeks after the UN-sanctioned invasion, the process of recovery was in full swing. Engineering robots cleaned the battlefield of damaged equipment and unexploded ordnance and set about repairing damaged infrastructure. Diplomatic Officers were sent into the field to address humanitarian needs and political reconciliation.

Diplomatic Officer Amanda Huygens rode her FCV-30 Forward Control Vehicle into the seemingly deserted village of Saya and dismounted. Her cotton uniform blouse fluttered in the gentle breeze as she scanned her environment. Saya was a single street tribal village far off the beaten path.

Known to be sympathetic to Homeland Guard insurgents, the village had been under close observation since the initiation of hostilities. As the first American on the scene, Amanda had been sent to assess the humanitarian needs of the village and render assistance as needed.

Her Army GuardBot escort team scurried and hovered ahead, investigating the road, the buildings, and obstacles along the road. Amanda's retinal scan indicated that the path to the local tribal chieftain's concrete and tin house was clear. Reminders of local etiquette scrolled across her lens as her heightened senses strained to hear any impending danger.

Knocking on the door, she called out, "Yo soy un diplomático de los Estados Unidos. Estoy aquí bajo orden 235 de la O.N.U." Her universal translator converted her West Texas drawl into a reasonable facsimile of rural Chuntu. A tall man in his early 40s answered the door. As he extended his right hand in a gesture of friendship, the Army GuardBot closest to her detected an added weight in his left. As a machete came into view, the GuardBot overrode its standing rules of engagement and sprayed the chieftain with 1,000 paralytic microflechettes, instantly bringing him to his knees.

An Army colonel, overseeing the escort operation from Colorado, reacquired control over the GuardBot and cautioned the chieftain through the GuardBot's onboard translator not to struggle and the effects of the drugs would be reversed. Instead, the chieftain began to subvocalize a command to his home communication network. The colonel twitched his eye and the microflechettes anesthetized the chieftain completely. He then commanded the rest of the robotic escort team to jam communications and lock down the house.

He quickly saw however that he had been too late. The message must have gotten out, because almost immediately he began to pick up a feed from nearby aerial surveillance drones that a group of vehicles violating curfew were heading towards the village. Microbots dispersed throughout the battlespace, hitched a ride on the vehicles and determined their armament, confirming their hostile intent according to the rules of engagement and the announced curfew. Amanda, reviewing the sitrep in coordination with intelligence and diplomatic officers, stood by as the colonel sent a real-time request for a military strike against the convoy. With no override order coming from Washington, the request was passed to a circling UCAV squadron, which carried out a high-energy laser strike within 5 minutes of the initial sighting.

Amanda leaned over the chieftain and wondered at his reaction. Surely, by now he would have understood the complete dominance of U.S. forces. He should know that she was only there to provide his people aid and a chance at a fresh start. She shivered at the thought of the machete, not wanting to be the war's first American casualty. She got back up and signaled to the rear humanitarian group to send forward the robotic reconstruction convoy and the standard class 3 rural supply package.

Discussion.

- How will military, intelligence, and diplomatic branches interoperate (or even merge) if diplomatic officials are the only Americans on the ground in war zones?
- What will be the role of the soldier if the battlefield is dominated by unmanned intelligent robotic combat and sensor systems?
- How much freedom of action should autonomous robots have on the future battlefield?
- How will coordination and decisionmaking occur when decision cycles are measured in minutes, seconds, or even microseconds? How does this impact the chain of command?

- How will coordination and decisionmaking occur when local decisionmaking can be overseen in real time from around the world?
- How would less-than-lethal weapons change the nature of warfare and postwar reconstruction?
- What are the international legal and political implications of a graduated approach to less-than-lethal and lethal force? Would its use constitute torture?

Scenario 6: Who Holds the High Ground.

In this scenario, we envision major competitive changes in the Earth-Moon system from the perspective of a traditional interagency space working group.

It is hard to put a finger on just when the land grab for the moon began. It might have begun with the arrival of private lunar rovers. At first, these companies made money by giving internet users an opportunity to remotely navigate the lunar surface from the privacy of their own dens. After several rovers were driven off cliffs, the owners reorganized to make money by claiming lunar real estate for those willing to buy an unenforceable deed and pay a continuing "maintenance of claim" fee.

The land grab might also be timed to the arrival of permanent moon bases by China, Russia, India, Brazil, the Islamic Republic, and the European Union (EU). Yet, these bases and their declared "territorial buffer zones" still occupied only a small percentage of the lunar surface.

Regardless of when the land grab began, it took off in earnest with the development of second-generation fusion reactors on Earth, which used Helium-3 as fuel.

He-3 deposits were known to be more abundant and accessible on the moon than on Earth.

Almost immediately, the moon bases began to send out rovers to test the lunar soil for He-3. The Group, a shadowy consortium of transnational corporations and wealthy individuals from all corners of the globe, seeing the potential for cornering a major new fuel market, bought their own passage to the moon and set up large-scale industrial strip mining operations, visible from Earth.

Despite a strong outcry by lunar environmentalists and poets alike, the Earth's unquenchable thirst for energy and the massive profits involved kept the pressure on to mine.

"If we don't get going soon, there won't be any place left for us to land!" exhaled Assistant Secretary Ted Benson of the Department of Commerce in exasperation.

"We shouldn't have left in the first place! We were sitting on a gold mine, and we didn't even know it," echoed Rascal Schwarski, NASA's Chief Engineering Officer.

"NASA had a choice to make, and you chose Mars and robotic space exploration instead of extending the useful life of the Asimov moon base," chided Dan Higgs, Deputy Undersecretary of Defense for Space Acquisition.

"Extending the moon base would have required an act of Congress. It doesn't matter how much you are authorized to spend, if they don't appropriate any funds!" Schwarski said defensively.

"Besides, we all know the DoD makes all the real funding decisions with Chairman Russell behind closed doors," added Schwarski.

"I wish that were so," chortled Dan. "Then, I wouldn't be sitting here with you knuckleheads every week for the past year trying to make a decision on the new space architecture."

"Can we all at least agree on a general goal, say 'return to the moon by 2045?'" pleaded Ross LaPorte, the President's Science Adviser. "We need to show some progress here."

"We won't have a launch system that can support that," Schwarski frowned. "The space elevator program award is still undergoing a challenge and won't come on line until at least 2050."

"I still don't understand why we can't just kill the elevator and take a low tech approach like our competitors," said the Commerce rep. "Or better yet, let's just buy commercial services."

"We've tried, but The Group has bought up all commercial flights for the next 20 years. I'm not sure if they need the flights or just want to keep us off the moon," said Schwarski.

The U.S. lead in space exploration and launch was lost as early as 2015, when China came online with its first hypervelocity sling. The mechanical "slingatron" allowed the Chinese to continuously hurl satellites and fuel for reusable launch vehicles to low Earth orbit (LEO). (It also provided China with a global conventional strike weapon.)

By 2020, other countries and companies, seeking to get to space on the cheap and tired of waiting on bureaucratic international collaboration efforts, bought their own slings and quickly began to fill LEO and later geosynchronous orbits with a host of satellites.

The United States did get to the moon in 2019, using the Constellation System, but the system was soon phased out as Moonbase Asimov was shut down, and the DoD chose to pursue its own new set of high-performance rockets.

The space elevator was going to be the long-term solution to the waning presence of America in space. A 60,000 mile high, carbon-fiber ladder to the stars, the elevator would dramatically lower costs to orbit and make space travel truly routine. And, unlike those crude slings, the elevator would be an engineering project for the ages. A new world wonder. An unprecedented achievement. The only problem was that they could not get it to work, and they could not get past the endless bid protests. The ten trillion dollar elevator would be a major contractor prize, if the General Accounting Office would just sanction an award.

"Can't you help NASA out with a few rides, Dan?" asked Presidential Adviser LaPorte.

"Our birds are focused on acquiring the remaining few geostationary orbits and defending our others from potential high energy laser anti-satellite weapon attacks. A number of EU satellites have been mysteriously winking out, when a Russian bird gets too close. Ross, we just don't have the capacity for a new mission," replied Higgs.

"Then I guess we table the discussion until our next weekly meeting. I trust you all will look for a solution with your internal process teams," prodded LaPorte. "Hopefully, we won't be looking at another recompete on the elevator."

Discussion.

- What is the national security role of space transportation and exploration?
- How will the emergence of a dynamic Earth-Moon system affect the roles and missions of the various U.S. departments and agencies?

- How should competing departmental interests and goals be managed? Can these goals be aligned with national goals?
- How will an increase in international and commercial space activities affect U.S. national space interests?
- How is public and congressional support for major, long-term space initiatives maintained?
- What should be the government role in developing and providing launch services?

Scenario 7: A Brave New World.

In this scenario, we examine a plan to apply proven neuroscience, psychiatric, and medical techniques to the control of pathological behaviors in a world of readily accessible weapons of mass destruction.

Colonel Samuel R. Wright, Commander Neuro-Psychological Operations, Special Forces Command, testified as follows before the Senate Global Relations Committee, Martinsville, West Virginia, June 14, 2040:

Colonel Wright: Ms. Chairwoman, Senator Wilkes, and Members of the Committee, I appreciate the opportunity to address you at this important moment in our history. The recent unfortunate release of classified mission information by the *Google Times* has compromised our efforts to help bring about the end of the threat of weapons of mass destruction in our time. I will not be able to go into detail about our mission in open session, but the general outlines are already well known. I would like to summarize my testimony and submit the full text for the record.

Chairwoman: Without objection, it will be received and added to the record. You may proceed, Colonel.

Colonel Wright: Thank you, Ms. Chairwoman. London. Jakarta. Beijing. Detroit. Sioux Falls. You all know the names. Cities that have been destroyed or made shadows of their former selves by terrorists and individuals seeking to wreak havoc on the rest of humanity.

London came first in 2012. A 15-kiloton improvised nuclear device detonated outside St. Paul's Cathedral. The remnants of Al Qaeda were suspected, but forensic evidence was inconclusive: 150,000 dead, 500,000 injured and diseased. 3,500 square miles contaminated.

A weapon with the same fingerprint killed another 200,000 in Jakarta just 2 years later. Again, many suspects, but nothing conclusive enough for retaliation.

In 2016, a modified form of the Bubonic Plague swept through Beijing, killing tens of thousands before burning itself out. The culprit: a disaffected 19-year-old medical student experimenting with a home biolab kit.

Detroit was abandoned in 2018, when radioactive cesium was found dispersed throughout the city. No one knew how it got there, and despite massive efforts by federal, state, and local agencies to clean up the city, the people decided not to return and the once great industrial and music hub Motown was no more.

After Detroit, the United States tightened border controls and immigration, but that did not stop the release of smallpox in Sioux Falls by an anarcho-environmentalist group seeking to rid the planet of the "human infection." Fortunately, a series of ring quarantines prevented a wider spread of the disease.

These major city attacks, as you know, have only been the tip of the iceberg. Suicide bombings and mass murders have become rampant in certain parts of the world. Ethnic cleansing occurs all too frequently in underdeveloped regions.

In the United States alone, attempts to bomb dams and nuclear power plants, poison public gathering places and farms, and destroy national landmarks grew throughout the 2020s. Advanced, ubiquitous public surveillance systems and expanded law enforcement prevented many great disasters.

The violent tide began to turn in the developed world, however, as unprecedented changes in the attitudes and behavior of the general population became manifest in the 2030s. These fundamental changes had been brought about quietly by advances in medical science and the development of a full understanding of the workings of the human mind.

Beginning in 2016, parents, who were already accustomed to eliminating genetic diseases from their unborn children, became enthusiastic supporters of new screening tests for the genetic and epigenetic markers of neurological disorders and violent pathological tendencies. How many parents want their kid to grow up to be the schoolyard bully or spend their adult life behind bars?

By 2030, the incidence of youth violence across the developed world showed a precipitous drop. It became clear that the vast majority of violent youth crime was being committed by a fairly small slice of the population, a part that had not been treated as children. New laws were enacted giving convicted adult felons the choice of incarceration or treatment. Recidivism rates became negligible among those treated.

Today, in the United States, in Europe, and in the Pacific Rim, we find ourselves in a new age of unprecedented peace and positive collaboration with all the benefits that entails. Like penicillin a century earlier, the so-called Healthy Mind and Body Revolution has changed personal and public health in ways that have yet to be counted.

Random acts of violence that had become common in the preceding decades have now all but disappeared in the developed world, which brings us back to the crisis we face today.

On April 23 of this year, the *Google Times* leaked details of Operation MERCY, causing it to be cut off prematurely. This covert operation was undertaken with the full consent of the UN Public Health and Bioethics Council and with the participation of our European and Asian allies.

As far back as the early 2020s, the World Health Organization has been using aerosol techniques to disperse vaccines and genetically modified viruses to treat many of the underdeveloped world's worst diseases. Operation MERCY's mission was to adapt these techniques to apply neuro-therapeutic measures to failed states around the world, starting with the Abbasid Republic. Not only has this pariah state refused to help its own people, it has been actively fueling racial and ideological hatred within its population through pharmacological means.

While historically we have often turned a blind eye to the internal affairs of sovereign nations, this fevered hatred, combined with the increasing accessibility of cheap, home kits for genetic engineering, chemical manufacture, and nanoparticle design, have made it essential for civilized nations to act. No longer can we tolerate individuals with bloodlust in their hearts and the means to create new, untold horrors in the privacy of their basements. How long do we have before one of these twisted, damaged souls unleashes a holocaust on this earth, one from which we cannot recover?

It is our duty to help these people, to bring them in from the cold. If their own governments will not help them, then we will. The *Google* leak will obviously make this task much harder. Already several nations are putting their nations on a war footing. It won't be easy to send vaccine-dispersal drones over these countries now, even for routine disease control. I ask that you support our efforts in this important public health initiative.

If you have questions, I'd be glad to answer them now.

Chairwoman: Thank you, Colonel Wright, for your testimony. As you know, we are on a short clock here this morning, so I think we should just jump right into questions. Let me begin by commending you on this important public service and your efforts to keep our nation safe. I, myself, lost a sister in Detroit. To put it bluntly, we are running out of time. The advancements in biology, chemistry, and nano-manufacturing over the last 2 decades have put the power to destroy civilization into the hands of people who cannot control themselves and hold only contempt for the rest of the world. Senator Wilkes?

Senator Wilkes: Thank you Ms. Chairwoman. Colonel Wright, what you are proposing is altering the minds of people you don't like against their will. How do you square this mission with the medical oath you took to "do no harm"?

Colonel Wright: These are people who already do not have a choice. Their governments are indoctrinating and drugging their children. Their economies are in collapse. They need our help.

Senator Wilkes: Colonel, the road to hell is paved with good intentions. Are we so arrogant as to believe our way is the right way?

Colonel Wright: If by "our way" you mean the approach adopted by leaders of both parties in closed session and by the UN and our allies, then yes, we do believe "our way" is the right way.

Senator Wilkes: But why, Colonel, did you feel the need to target the Middle East for your operation? Surely, there are unstable people in many parts of the world?

Colonel Wright: That is true, but there is a particular threat in that region. The Abbasid Republic has not recovered from the devastation and humiliation of the Second Yom Kippur War in 2027. While Israel lost Jerusalem and Haifa, all the major cities of the Abbasid Republic were destroyed in the nuclear exchange. Instead of turning outward for help, the Abbasid Republic turned inward, refusing aid and stoking resentments in their children.

While most of the rest of the world has chosen a path of growth and global community, the Abbasid Republic has retreated into poverty, corruption, and abuse. Right now, as I speak, their children are being trained for suicide missions. I do not think we can afford to find out where they will attack next.

Chairman: That buzzer is our final call for the floor vote on the motion to condemn this operation. Colonel, we will have to continue this another day. This meeting is adjourned.

Discussion.

- What is the role of government in controlling pathological and anti-social behavior worldwide?
- If we develop the capability to cure pathological behaviors, will we use it and how will we use it? What are the unintended consequences?

- How will pathological behavior be defined? Who will define it?
- What moral, ethical, and legal issues does this raise in regard to the U.S. population? . . . the world population?
- What would our response be to another country using these techniques to control their own population?
- How would we defend our own population against adversaries?
- What will be the role of law enforcement and the military if pathological behaviors are reduced or eliminated globally?
- How would the United States gather the necessary intelligence to determine the psychological health of a noncooperative foreign population?
- What would be the impact on the economy of a nonpathological, or even happy, populace?
- How would these changes affect the congressional committee structure and oversight functions of Congress?

2060

Scenario 8: A Warm Reception.

In this scenario, we focus on the challenge of developing international consensus for action on the issue of global climate and the possibility of unintended consequences.

Special Envoy Amanda Huygens stepped out on the balcony of the U.S. Embassy in New Delhi. The reception was in full swing inside and she needed to catch a breath of fresh air. As dusk gathered, she looked wistfully over the city towards the New India

Gate, rebuilt painstakingly after the war with Pakistan in 2038.

Tensions were building again now. The negotiations were not going as planned. In fact, all the simulations had proven wrong. The Bangladeshi foreign minister was being surprisingly stubborn and had found staunch allies in Canada and the Soviet Republic.

Despite decades of good intentions, as well as political posturing on the importance of "doing something" about global warming, nothing significant had been done. Yes, there were treaties that reduced the rate of growth of greenhouse emissions at the margins and new technologies that had raised the efficiencies of power generation and usage, but the growing prosperity (and the corresponding fossil fuel emissions) of Asia, Latin America, and more recently the Central African Union, had dwarfed these efforts.

"If the temperature rise just hadn't stalled in the first 2 decades of the 21st century," Amanda whispered to herself, "we could have resolved this years ago."

"That may be wishful thinking," chimed Marta, her "automated personal access liaison" or aPAL. "There is little evidence to suggest that there was any more political will to act in 2015 than there is today."

"Marta, you're such a cynic," thought Amanda. "Link me to the Director; we need to get back to work."

"The Director's assistant tells me that he is in conference. Do you wish to speak with his aPAL, Bobby?"

"Sure. . . . Bobby, is the Director going to be able to talk to the President today about our negotiating position on the latest dumping of fertilizers into the Indian Ocean? Tell him that we agree with the integrated value analysis by the U.S. Internal Climate Security

Working Group that shows that Bangledesh needs to be stopped soon."

In 2051, the Bangledeshi government had decided it had waited long enough for the world to act on global warming. Their country was 5 percent under water. Taking matters into their own hands, they started dumping thousands of tons of iron oxide and chemical fertilizers into the ocean with the intent to cause a massive algae bloom that would absorb excess CO_2 from the air and reverse rising temperatures. Instead, they were shocked to discover that their fertilization of the ocean had supercharged the regional ecological system with the effect of pumping into the atmosphere massive new amounts of methane—a greenhouse gas much more severe than CO_2.

The result was a sudden spike in global temperature. Gradual global melting that the world had largely ignored now became a torrent. Sea levels began to rise faster than coastal areas could respond, even in the wealthiest countries. Some major cities, like London; New York; Washington, DC; and Los Angeles struggled to hold back the sea. Other areas, such as the Netherlands and large parts of Florida, were abandoned to the sea.

The rising temperatures and shifts in regional climates had also dramatically affected agriculture and fisheries. Some areas had too much rain, others too little. Some had too long winters, others had too short. The loss of pollinating species alone had led to the collapse of local ecosystems and major famines. Social unrest and displacement were rampant, leading to conflicts around the globe.

Bangledesh itself by 2060 was inundated, losing 20 percent of its territory to rising waters. A steady surge of refugees tried to cross into neighboring countries, but was stopped by armed border guards. Still, Bangladesh did not stop the dumping. The crisis had finally gotten the world's attention, and it was intent to keep the pressure on.

"Excuse me, Amanda. The Canadian Ambassador has arrived for your party and has requested to see you," interrupted Marta.

Ambassador, welcome to the Embassy. Enjoy the refreshments. I'll be with you shortly, thought Amanda. "Marta, what's your analysis of convincing the Ambassador to accept a blockade of Bangledeshi ships?"

"One moment please while I access the U.S. Atmospheric Carbon Sequestration Agency and coordinate with State, Defense, and Intelligence. . . . I project low confidence that the Ambassador will change his position. Canadian oil, gas, and mineral interests in the newly thawed regions of the Arctic, combined with the increasing probability that Canada will become the breadbasket of the world over the next 20 years, argues for continued opposition."

"I guess that leaves us with the joint EU/Pan-Asia proposal to launch a 2,000-mile-wide solar parasol to shade the Earth directly," sighed Amanda. "Do you think the Canadians would go along with that?"

"I estimate similar opposition by the Canadians, but I have high confidence that they will not directly interfere. There is a strong risk, however, that the Soviets will shoot the parasol down," assessed Marta.

Discussion.

- What will be the role of national security in addressing global commons issues?
- What are the limits of national sovereignty when the "commons" are threatened?

- How should environmental matters be addressed in a national security framework?
- How can the United States achieve its international goals if international organizations cannot reach consensus to act?
- With the aid of real-time networking and intelligent assistants, will gaining the President's attention be the chief limiting factor to decision-making?

Scenario 9: It's a Small World.

In this scenario, we explore the implications of a very different future, wherein small, molecular scale machines (nanotechnology robots or "nanobots") have become ubiquitous.

In 2037, the age of nanotech almost came to a screeching halt when unmoderated, self-replicating nanobots escaped accidentally from a design plant and converted a large chunk of the outskirts of Mexico City into gray slag.

The so-called "gray goo" expanded from the plant in an ever increasing arc of destruction as each individual nanobot reproduced itself thousands of times per second using the raw materials available in the soil, roads, and buildings of Mexico City.

After several attempts at stopping the nanobot ooze, high-temperature thermite bombs were dropped to create a firebreak and all of the nanobots were vaporized. Unfortunately, the resulting citywide conflagration continued the devastation that the nanobots had begun.

Looking back, it was still hard for United States CFO Miranda Chavez to understand how this transformative event had led to a global political movement to ban the continued development of nanotechnology. These "neo-Luddites," as they came to be called, thought only about the downside of these new technologies and always in the bleakest possible light. The fact that the gray goo event had not gobbled up the entire globe as most neo-Luddites had predicted, did not seem to moderate their views in the slightest: "If you can't see it, you shouldn't build it" was their unofficial motto.

Only the inexorable demand by consumers for new products and new cures and the need of business for new products to sell staved off a tidal wave of reaction against these invisible machines. Three years later, the movement disbanded, only to be reborn a decade later to call attention to the rise in nanobot and bioorganic smog.

The smog was the result of the undeclared Nano Wars of 2045-52. Miranda had been only a teenager when the war broke out or rather bubbled to the surface.

To feed the growing resource needs of the early nanofabrication industry, some companies had decided to send small nanobots into the world's oceans to scavenge for heavy metals, rare earth elements, and certain naturally occurring molecules. Larger nanobots and microscopic robots would then collect the fully loaded scavenger nanobots and bring them back for processing.

The trouble began in 2040, when coastal governments around the world began to complain that minerals were being harvested from their territorial waters. The complaints, however, went nowhere because the scavenger companies were careful to leave no identifying marks on their equipment.

Finally, the Japanese government took matters into its own hands and granted the first privateering charters to its own nanotech companies, allowing them to send out nanobots to scavenge other companies' nanobots found in Japanese territorial waters.

Other countries quickly followed suit, sending out their own nanobot patrols. Some of these patrols extended their reach beyond their own territorial waters, forcing even responsible nanotech corporations to add protective capabilities to their own nanobots.

The ensuing global free-for-all filled the oceans with an entire new ecology of nanoscale robotics and synthetic biological creatures in a continuous life and death struggle unknown to the natural life forms that continued to thrive in parallel.

In 2052, the International League of Democracies agreed to a set of guiding principles for scavenging and released its own nanobots into the ocean to police the worst offenders. This force was dubbed "the blue goo."

Since that time, global nano competition had extended beyond the oceans and into the earth's crust. Governments followed with additional guiding principles, regulations, and laws fashioned to keep subterranean nano-miners from undercutting houses, sewers, and feedstock lines and from draining natural aquifers.

Finally, nanobots and synthetic bioorganisms had been introduced to the air. At first this was a defensive effort to watch for and contain biological or nanotechnology attacks. Later it became a means to increase natural immunities and pass health treatments among the population, like iodine had been added to salt and fluoride to water. Eventually, just as in the oceans and under the earth, the air hosted a constant and relentless struggle between good particles and bad.

Miranda half expected the nano competition to extend someday into space, but it was of no concern to her. On occasion she had smelled a faint miasma, the results of a skirmish too small to see, or she would trip on a small sinkhole that had yet to be repaired. But again, this was a small price to pay for a world without hunger, poverty, disease, and aging, all thanks to the everyday miracles of nano production.

Miranda had taken a leading role in licensing nano assemblers to make the basic human necessities freely available worldwide through a consortium of industrial and religious organizations. Simultaneously, global competition ensured the spread of more sophisticated nano production facilities worldwide, making even luxury goods available for a song.

The efficiencies of nanotechnology had brought the cost of most goods down below the former price of the constituent raw materials. Nano production required significantly less energy than traditional macroscopic production and resulted in no appreciable waste. The need for transportation was also largely eliminated by the ability to make products just about anywhere.

Nano businesses primarily made their money through creating new and more fashionable products. Older designs were quickly copied and made available for free to anyone on the mesh network.

Real estate was the only remaining high priced good, and even that was changing now as the nano industry honed its ability to design and "grow" new land out of the sea floor and in less hospitable regions of the world. Deserts and tundra alike were becoming paradisiacal oases, for the right price.

Discussion.

- How will government be redefined in a world of ubiquitous nanotechnology?

- Will nations seek to control nanotechnology to forestall economic or military rivals?
- Will there be any "great powers"?
- Will traditional militaries be replaced by molecular machines?
- What will be the role of the military, police, and intelligence in a world where every cubic inch contains myriad sensing and surveillance devices?
- How will diplomacy change in a world without a need for trade?
- Is there a role for economic sanctions when most things are made locally and at almost no cost?
- What form of government will be needed in a world of plenty?
- Will anyone work in a world where basic needs are met for free?
- What will be of value in a world of free products?
- Is it possible to balance the benefits of nanotechnology with their impact on the environment?

A SPECIAL NOTE ON THE POSSIBILITY OF A TECHNOLOGICAL SINGULARITY BY 2060

The authors of this set of scenarios have intentionally omitted any scenarios driven by what has been dubbed a "technological singularity" or, more grandiosely, "The Singularity." Several technologists estimate a singularity occurring within the period covered by these scenarios. Although there are many definitions, in general, a technological singularity is said to occur when intentional, intelligent machines take over their own development, and due to their superior memories and processing abilities, quickly advance to states beyond human comprehension. It is hypothesized that such superintelligent entities will reshape the world as they see fit, with or without human input.

The decision to omit a singularity scenario was based on practicality, rather than a determination that such a scenario is implausible. The range of post-Singularity predictions is too broad and speculative to be of use in the current job of rewriting the 1947 National Security Act in 2008. If a singularity occurs and humanity, in some form, survives, it may be time then to revisit the question of interagency cooperation and communication on national security affairs. For now, we will simply note the possibility in the interest of inclusiveness.

CHAPTER 4

THE NINE POST-REFORM SCENARIOS

Chris Waychoff
Matthew Russell

2020
Impact on Scenario 1: Red Death
Impact on Scenario 2: People's War
Impact on Scenario 3: A Grand Strategy

2040
Impact on Scenario 4: A New Economy
Impact on Scenario 5: Pax Robotica
Impact on Scenario 6: Who Holds the High Ground
Impact on Scenario 7: A Brave New World

2060
Impact on Scenario 8: A Warm Reception
Impact on Scenario 9: It's a Small World

2020

Impact on Scenario 1: Red Death.

In the original scenario, we met a country struggling to get back on its feet after a major biological attack and witnessed a debate about the future role of the U.S. Government both at home and abroad. In the update to the scenario, measures have been put into place to prevent such an attack.

Dr. Meishan Prosper, MD, ScD, pulled into the driveway of the Centers for Disease Control (CDC) in Atlanta, still puzzling over the last meeting of the Bioterror Interagency Team. An al Qaeda splinter group was trying its hardest to infect world leaders with homemade biological agents using locally infected diplomats as carriers. They kept trying despite the seeming futility of such efforts.

Three attempts had been made in the last 6 months resulting only in the deaths of some low-level Iranian and Syrian diplomats who had not been treated in time. These officials had become the unwitting pawns in a deadly global game of move—countermove. Apparently, the terrorists hadn't gotten the word that U.S. and allied officials were now protected by several layers of sophisticated sensing and detection devices developed by private industry and Argonne National Laboratory, so small as to be hardly noticeable. The very fabric of the President's and his advisers' clothes was treated to both detect and destroy airborne and contact pathogens.

The air at the White House, State Department, United Nations (UN), and other diplomatic meeting spots was constantly circulated through filters with sensors and tested for old and new viruses, bacteria, and prions. New agents were neutralized and gene sequenced, and their composition transmitted to labs around the world in real time, including here at the CDC.

Dr. Prosper and her team were three for three in identifying, neutralizing, and developing treatment protocols for the attacks. Still, the terrorists might just get lucky someday.

She voice activated her car's view-screen and patched in the team. "We need to do some more gaming on possible infiltration scenarios. I'm worried that we might be missing something, that these attacks might be lulling us into a sense of complacency."

Colonel Andrews out of Fort Detrick, Maryland, responded, "Let's do that. I'll set it up with the National Assessment & Visioning Center. We should bring in the unexamined threats team to generate some unconventional inputs into the game."

Impact on Scenario 2: People's War.

In the original scenario, the United States faced global asymmetric warfare against a nuclear-armed great power. The entire Federal Government was caught in the conundrum of how to respond to anonymous attacks at home and abroad while avoiding an escalation to nuclear war. In the update to the scenario, the national security interagency process enables a better-informed and agile interagency response.

When National Security Professional Corps Intelligence Specialist Robert Wong worked the wall, the entire room paid attention. He was a blur of motion as he pulled up information on the latest fleet situational reports, news reports and broadcasts of domestic assassinations and sabotage, and statistical analyses of the likelihood that these were isolated events. It was hard to argue with the picture he painted: the United States was in a global, undeclared war with China.

The truce following the triumph of the U.S. Pacific Fleet over the Chinese incursion had apparently been empty rhetoric on the part of Chairman Tang. China had claimed that the surprise attack on Taiwan was an internal matter and that U.S. forces had accidentally gotten in the way. Specialist Wong showed that the Chinese had never taken the truce seriously and had not hesitated to continue its war by other means.

Based on this analysis, General Garzoff, the Chair of Interagency Crisis Task Force Gold, sanctioned a Red Homeland Alert under the National Operational Framework and patched in the President's Director of National Security to recommend that the President be briefed on options to raise the national defense posture and protect U.S. supply chains and interests overseas. Garzoff then triggered the Business Emergency Management Assistance Compact to release additional government assets to help companies fight the information assault on their systems.

After a brief video conference with the President and his Director of National Security, Garzoff ordered a restructuring of the Gold Team. Strategic nuclear and conventional warfighting issues would be managed directly by the President through the traditional combatant commands, supported by a new Silver Team that would provide connectivity to the other agencies and the Gold Team.

Asymmetric warfare would become the primary focus of the Gold Team, which would be expanded to include additional affected agencies, such as the Departments of Transportation, Energy, and the Treasury. The Gold Team would have three subordinate teams, one working defensive operations, one working offensive strategy, and the other coordinating Chinese-U.S. negotiations. State Department negotiators would coordinate their efforts with both the Gold and Silver Teams going forward. The Director of National Security through General Garzoff would bridge the two Teams. Intelligence Specialist Wong was rewarded for his keen insights by taking the lead of the Gold Team's offensive strategy development.

Impact on Scenario 3: A Grand Strategy.

In the original scenario, we explored the utility of an integrated grand strategy development capability for smoothing the transition from one presidential administration to another. This update to the scenario required only modest revisions to accord with a post-PNSR world.

President-Elect Anne Cummings stepped down into the well of the large conference room with her entourage. The lush blue carpet and warm wooden panels created a hushed effect, almost like entering an old library or a church. A bird fluttered across the oval skylight. Was that real sky? she wondered.

Tom Hughes, the Director of the National Assessment and Visioning Center, strode across the carpet and extended his hand. "Welcome back, Governor. We are honored to have you here today."

"It is my pleasure, Tom. It's good to see you again in person. It's been a couple years since we held the Governors Convention here," she said with a warm smile. "You know Dr. Tyrone Chandra, my national security advisor; Ms. Catalina Sharp, my economic advisor; and Ms. Akemi Takahashi, my long-range planner?"

"Yes, good to see you all again. Akemi has been working very closely with us and her predecessor to refine the underlying model assumptions. I'm happy to say that not much tweaking was necessary. We paid pretty close attention to the campaign, " beamed the Director.

"I'd also like to welcome the folks conferencing in," the Director said, indicating the faces strung out along the top edge of the screen that wrapped floor-to-ceiling 270° around the conference room. "We are pleased to have your transition liaisons join us from the various department strategy offices, along with senior representatives of the outgoing Simpson administration. Welcome all."

"My mission today is to acquaint you with the general operation of the National Assessment and Visioning Center and its departmental satellite offices," announced the Director.

"NAVC was first funded in 2009 to assist the President and his administration in developing a dynamic national grand strategy. The ability to create such a strategy was complicated by interagency stovepipes and rice bowls, political constraints on free and open discussion, and the technical difficultly of developing an integrated strategy in an increasingly complicated and interconnected world.

"The hope for the new organization was that it would not only be a safe place to debate, develop, test, and monitor long-range strategies, but that it could be an objective source of information that could withstand a change in administration. The problem, of course, was that pure objectivity was a mirage. Despite the best intentions and the selection of generally open-minded staff, bias and ideology always crept back in.

"The answer was to embrace varying points of view . . . to model and evaluate all points of view, rather than trying to find the one correct view," continued the Director.

"As I hope Akemi has told you, our bipartisan, or rather multipartisan, process is now ensured through our agency's host of checks and balances. These measures touch on all our activities ranging from how we hire and rotate our staff to how we build our models and debate the results.

"We also found that an open process keeps us honest, so we have developed an extensive outreach process to participants across the political spectrum, in government, industry, and academia. Our public discussion boards are particularly lively–there is nothing some posters like better than catching us with an unsupported assumption or an incorrect application of an algorithm," chuckled the Director.

"So are all points of view deemed to be of equal value and effectiveness?" asked Dr. Chandra, the incoming national security advisor.

"I wouldn't put it that way. While all points of view are captured and modeled, their value and effectiveness are determined by many other factors within the modeling system. Positions must be supported by evidence and coherent, logical paths. If they are simply assertions, they will be flagged as such," replied the Director. "Why don't we look at an example?"

Swiping the screen of his wristwatch, the Director brought the main wall to animated life as a timeline stretched from 1980 at one end to 2080 at the other.

"Let's run a quick 'what if' scenario," said the Director as he walked to a large, inclined touchscreen table in the center of the room. Waving his hand over a world map, he highlighted the countries of the nascent Latin American Union. The main wall glowed with event and trend markers in a rainbow of colors.

"This view here is as close to a normative, objective view as we can produce. As you see, it's pretty sparse and contains only elements that are demonstrable, accepted facts or trends that have been broadly agreed upon within the statistical boundaries indicated."

"If we call up your administration's view," the Director said as he subvocalized a command to the wall, "we see there is much more detail at this level. We can also cycle through the department views . . . notice the intersections where one department's strategy runs into another department's."

"What are the flashing icons?" asked Dr. Chandra.

"The flashing icons represent new elements that have been placed on the wall by the system's estimation engine, but have not yet been validated by our team members. This one here is an analysis by the State Department's Latin America Desk of General Secretary Chávez's recent address to the LAU General Assembly. As you can see, if I tap on the icon there is a complete interagency argument map supporting the analysis, plus a video of the speech."

"Do you get a feed of all operational and intelligence information?" quizzed Dr. Chandra.

"No, we don't here. Downstairs we have a parallel center that takes our feed behind the Common Secured Environment firewall and integrates it with classified, sensitive, and operational information. Up here, we are neither an operations center nor an intelligence fusion center. We are strictly an open source, meta-analysis center, integrating the best analysis of our government and public partners. We find that what we lose in not having access to the latest classified information is compensated for by our ability to have an open dialogue with a wide variety of experts and stakeholders. Moreover, our timeline is a little longer. We are not overwhelmed by the day's in-basket. We have the luxury, as well as the responsibility, to look longer term."

"Can we look at the trends from an economic point of view?" queried the President-elect's economic advisor.

"Certainly. Here are your administration's economic trend lines under the 'what if' assumption that Mexico joins the LAU embargo of oil to the United States."

"What is that red line receding into the background?" she asked.

"That indicates a strong connection between this economic scenario and domestic politics in the U.S. Southwest," the Director replied.

"Have you gotten to the point where the grand strategy writes itself?" joked the President-Elect.

"Hah, hah, no, no, the primary job of the models, analysis, and visualizations you have seen is to get our collective thinking organized. There are too many options, too many impacts, too many interrelationships for the human mind to follow without assistance.

"The Center and its partner centers in each agency help avoid continually reinventing the wheel and arguing past one another. The real work, the work of finding common ground, crafting solutions, and implementing these solutions to achieve national objectives begins only here with your people, aided by our staff. Decisionmaking remains the domain of the President and Congress."

2040

Impact on Scenario 4: A New Economy.

In the original scenario, the United States faced its worst economic crisis since the Great Depression. The crisis was a perfect storm of the unintended consequences of new technologies, policies, court decisions, and popular expectations. In this update, government, industry, and the public work together to find solutions to a new economic reality.

Ron Guilder laid back in his favorite arm chair, which shifted to better conform to his thin frame. Ron knew the meeting did not start for another 5 minutes, but he always arrived early to meetings and could not help himself. This despite the fact that he knew others on the Homeland Security Collaboration Subcommittee were equally susceptible to being 10 minutes late.

Ron liked to complain about the virtual meetings, how sometimes they were tedious and how they took up all his time, but secretly he looked forward to the meetings. They gave him purpose, something to do. And he knew they were important.

Ron had been the Chief Financial Officer of a Fortune 500 company before automated intelligent enterprise systems and robots made him obsolete. Like others, at first he had embraced his new life of early retirement and leisure.

Robotic manufacturing and intelligent management systems had streamlined business, lowering prices on goods and services to the point where everyone had the basics, plus most luxuries too.

Ron, however, suspected that no work and all play would make him and everyone else a dull boy, so he was grateful when his name came up to participate in a regional economic subcommittee of the Homeland Security Collaboration Committee. The subcommittee worked with committees across the country networked through the federal collaborative information knowledge management system. Their mission: figure out how to maintain a healthy, productive, and free society with nearly unlimited wealth and leisure and few opportunities for employment.

The arguments at times were fairly heated. Some advocated a laissez faire approach, maximizing individual freedom and minimizing government intervention. Others took an opposite tack, arguing for a greater government role. The most extreme holders of this view thought the government needed to get people off their couches, unhook them from their varied electronic forms of nirvana, and force to them to improve themselves through education and art projects.

The greatest thing about these discussions was that the entire debate was captured and analyzed by an intelligent assistant. It noted when lines of argument were duplicated, when they violated previously argued positions, and when evidence was lacking. This meant that the meetings actually made progress, that nonsense could be discarded, and that common ground might ultimately be found.

Ron's concerns were focused on economic issues. He was worried that the new economic realities were unprecedented and hence unpredictable. He worried that life right now was a little too good to be true. He shared his views with like-minded individuals, who got him started modeling his concerns and then expanded his group to include others who thought him a Malthusian pessimist. The result was a vigorous, quantitative debate that seemed to be making headway. In fact, some of their findings last year had helped undermine a U.S. Supreme Court case urging a constitutional right to food and shelter. More recently, their work made its way into a revision of the Income Preservation Act of 2034.

Ah, well, since the meeting was going to start late anyway, Ron decided to grab a quick bite to eat. With a series of rapid eye movements and guttural remarks Ron ordered his home robotic system to bring him a nice vat-grown pastrami sandwich made from that 14-grain artisan rye bread he enjoyed so much.

Impact on Scenario 5: Pax Robotica.

In the original scenario, we explored the intersection of unmanned robotic warfare and on-the-ground diplomacy. This scenario depended upon the continuation of current accelerating trends in robotics and sensors technology, as well as a public policy choice to enable greater real-time interaction between the military, diplomatic, and intelligence arms of the U.S. government. In this update to the scenario, more authority for postwar operations is granted to a strengthened Department of State that now includes all nonmilitary functions of foreign affairs.

Total dominance of the battlefield had been achieved in just 3 days. From command bunkers in Colorado, override controllers watched as autonomous robotic swarms annihilated the loyalist Homeland Guard with minimal collateral damage. The remainder of the Chuntu Army saw what was coming, listened to the broadcast warnings, dropped their weapons, and ran home as fast as they could. The genocidal Chuntu leadership was captured or killed in brief, but brutal, house-to-house fighting with wheeled, crawling, and airborne robots.

Now, 2 weeks after the UN-sanctioned invasion, the process of recovery was in full swing. U.S. Department of Defense engineering robots cleaned the battlefield of damaged equipment and unexploded ordnance, while State Department robots set about repairing damaged infrastructure. Diplomatic Officers were sent into the field to address humanitarian needs and political reconciliation.

Diplomatic Officer Amanda Huygens rode her FCV-30 Forward Control Vehicle into the seemingly deserted village of Saya and dismounted. Her cotton uniform blouse fluttered in the gentle breeze as she scanned her environment. Saya was a single street tribal village far off the beaten path.

Known to be sympathetic to Homeland Guard insurgents, the village had been under close observation since the initiation of hostilities. As the first American on the scene, Amanda had been sent to assess the humanitarian needs of the village and render assistance as needed.

Her Army GuardBot escort team scurried and hovered ahead, investigating the road, the buildings, and obstacles along the road. Amanda's retinal scan indicated that the path to the local tribal chieftain's concrete and tin house was clear. Reminders of local etiquette scrolled across her lens as her heightened senses strained to hear any impending danger.

Knocking on the door, she called out "Yo soy un diplomático de los Estados Unidos. Estoy aquí bajo orden 235 de la O.N.U." Her universal translator converted her West Texas drawl into a reasonable facsimile of rural Chuntu. A tall man in his early 40s answered the door. As he extended his right hand in an apparent gesture of friendship, the Army GuardBot closest to her detected an added weight in his left. As a machete came into view, the GuardBot overrode its standing rules of engagement and sprayed the chieftain with 1,000 paralytic microflechettes, instantly bringing him to his knees.

An Army colonel, overseeing the escort operation from Colorado, reacquired control over the GuardBot and cautioned the chieftain through the GuardBot's onboard translator not to struggle, and the effects of the drugs would be reversed. Instead, the chieftain began to subvocalize a command to his home communication network. The colonel twitched his eye, and the microflechettes anaesthetized the chieftain completely. The colonel then commanded the rest of the robotic escort team to jam communications and lock down the house.

However, the colonel quickly saw that he had been too late. The message must have gotten out, because almost immediately he began to pick up a feed from nearby aerial surveillance drones that a group of vehicles violating curfew were heading towards the village. Microbots dispersed throughout the battlespace, hitched a ride on the vehicles and determined their armament, confirming their hostile intent according to the rules of engagement and the announced curfew.

Amanda, reviewing the situation report in coordination with intelligence and diplomatic officers, stood by as the colonel sent a real-time request for a military strike against the convoy. With no override order coming from Amanda or Washington, the request was passed to a circling UCAV squadron, which carried out a high-energy laser strike within five minutes of the initial sighting.

Amanda leaned over the chieftain and wondered at his reaction. Surely, by now he would have understood the complete dominance of U.S. forces. He should know that she was there only to provide his people aid and a chance at a fresh start. She shivered at the thought of the machete, not wanting to be the war's first American casualty. She straightened herself and signaled to the rear humanitarian group to send forward the robotic reconstruction convoy and the standard class 3 rural supply package. The tribal leader was now the colonel's responsibility.

Impact on Scenario 6: Who Holds the High Ground.

In the original scenario, we envisioned major competitive changes in the Earth-Moon system from the perspective of a traditional interagency space working group. In this updated scenario, a standing Interagency Team has been formed to bridge differences in agency priorities.

It is hard to put a finger on just when the Moon became so important, but the trend lines were clearly visible in the long-range forecasts of the National Assessment and Visioning Center. Based on a strategic review of these trends in 2010, the President's Security Council ordered the formation of a standing Interagency Team, dubbed Team Eagle.

The Team was designed to navigate the shoals of competing agency priorities and make unified recommendations to the Office of Management and Budget for funding in the National Security Resource Document, the rolling integrated national security resource strategy. It included all the usual suspects: representatives from the Department of Defense, the Office of the Director of National Intelligence, NASA, NOAA, and the Department of Commerce. This traditional group was augmented by the Assistants for National Security for Energy, State, and Treasury once deposits of Helium-3 were found on the Moon.

He-3, the fuel of second-generation fusion reactors on Earth, was the first significant resource found in outer space. Available in abundance on the lunar surface, it provoked a land grab among countries and companies alike.

Realizing the strategic importance of this development, Team Eagle developed a two-track strategy to modernize its space transportation system and to negotiate a global treaty on shared access to lunar resources. China, Russia, India, Brazil, the Islamic Republic, the European Union, and a private consortium called simply The Group all had Moon bases these days and were looking for a better path than a dangerous land grab.

"What's the status of the latest round of negotiations?" queried Assistant for National Security Ted Benson of the Department of Commerce.

"Most of the delegations are on board with the latest draft, but Brazil is still holding out for a larger stake," reported Rascal Schwarski, NASA's Chief Engineering Officer.

"I think it's just a matter of time before they agree," offered Dan Higgs, Deputy Undersecretary of Defense for Space Acquisition. "Let's turn our attention to securing our launch capacity. Space elevator construction is well underway, but we have a disagreement over cislunar and translunar transportation. We need the capability to put objects into geosynchronous and Lagrangian orbits. NASA is focused on Asimov Moon-base resupply and a run at Mars."

"Congress is not in the mood to fund two solutions," Schwarski said defensively.

"That's why we need to work together to form a win-win proposition that is too good for Congress to ignore." offered Ross LaPorte, the Special Assistant for Space to the Director of National Security. Ross was a member of the National Security Professional Corps and a recent detailee from the Office of Science and Technology Policy. Ross chaired Team Eagle and sought ways to break through roadblocks wherever they occurred.

"I think if we can model our solutions in the context of the changing strategic environment, we will have a better chance of convincing Chairman Russell and his House Select National Security Committee on Space of the importance of space in the coming decades," continued LaPorte. "We need to show him the tangible economic benefits of moving forward and national security costs of standing still. He's a patriot and concerned for his constituents. If we can make the case, I think he'll make the appropriate decision."

Impact on Scenario 7: A Brave New World.

In this scenario, we examined a plan to apply proven neuroscience, psychiatric, and medical techniques to the control of pathological behaviors in a world of readily accessible weapons of mass destruction. In this update to the scenario, the National Operational Framework, the National Security Planning Guidance, and the National Security Resource Document have provided the foundation for keeping the United States and its allies free from severe terror attacks for several decades; however, modeling in the National Assessment and Visioning Center reveals that an attack from the underdeveloped world will eventually get through if the underlying neuro-psychological conditions are not addressed.

Colonel Samuel R. Wright, Chair, Neuro-Psychological Health Interagency Team, testified as follows before the Senate Select National Security Committee for Neuro-Psychological Operations, Washington, DC, June 14, 2040.

Colonel Wright: Ms. Chairwoman, Senator Wilkes, and Members of the Committee, I appreciate the opportunity to address you at this important moment in our history. I would like to summarize my testimony and submit the full text for the record.

Chairwoman: Without objection, it will be received and added to the record. You may proceed, Colonel.

Colonel Wright: Thank you, Ms. Chairwoman. I come before you today with a proposal to end global conflict and violence. In the United States, in Europe, and in the Pacific Rim, we find ourselves in an age of unprecedented peace and positive collaboration, with all the benefits that entails. Like penicillin a century earlier, the so-called Healthy Mind and Body Revolution has changed personal and public health in ways that have yet to be counted.

We in the administration believe it is time to share this miracle of modern science with the rest of the world, the part of the world that still suffers from casual violence, that still threatens violence against its neighbors, the source of terrorist attacks that continue to this day.

As you are well aware, beginning in 2016, parents, who were already accustomed to eliminating genetic diseases from their unborn children, became enthusiastic supporters of new screening tests for the genetic and epigenetic markers of neurological disorders and violent pathological tendencies. How many parents want their kid to grow up to be the schoolyard bully or spend their adult life behind bars?

By 2030, the incidence of youth violence across the developed world showed a precipitous drop. It became clear that the vast majority of violent youth crime was being committed by a fairly small slice of the population, a part that had not been treated as children. New laws were enacted giving convicted adult felons the choice of incarceration or treatment. Recidivism rates became negligible among those treated.

This dramatic change in human motivation combined with sophisticated policing and ubiquitous terror detection technology has largely ended the threats within our borders, but this is not the case in the underdeveloped parts of the world.

You know the history. A 15-kiloton improvised nuclear device destroyed Chittagong, Bangladesh's main seaport, in 2012, leaving 100,000 dead and injured. A weapon with the same fingerprint killed another 200,000 in Jakarta just two years later.

In 2016, a modified form of the Bubonic Plague swept through San'a, the capital of Yemen, killing tens of thousands before burning itself out. The culprit: a disaffected 19-year-old medical student experimenting with a home biolab kit.

Radiological attacks in Mandalay, Burma, and Harare, Zimbabwe, led to few deaths, but mass panic and abandonment of those cities. Neither government had the wherewithal or motivation to clean them up.

These major city attacks, as you know, have only been the tip of the iceberg. Suicide bombings and mass murders have become rampant in certain parts of the world. Ethnic cleansing occurs all too frequently in underdeveloped regions.

Which brings us to the proposal before you today. Working with your staff, the Neuro-Psychological Health Interagency Team has developed a three-point plan to end the scourge of violence from the Earth once and for all.

First, we propose that the United States work with the UN Public Health and Bioethics Council and our European and Asian allies to establish the goal of 100 percent national participation in a new Operation MERCY before the decade is out.

Second, Operation MERCY will establish a common global fund to assist poor countries in setting up neuro-psychological treatment centers in hospitals and prison facilities. This fund will depend upon national aid programs and private donations.

Third, we propose that the UN develop contingency plans for inoculating the populations of any pariah nation that does not voluntarily participate in the program and continues to try to export terror, threaten foreign invasion, or terrorizes its own populace. We will use the same aerosol dispersion techniques the

World Health Organization has been using for the past two decades to distribute vaccines and genetically modified viruses to treat many of the underdeveloped world's worst diseases.

While historically we have often turned a blind eye to the internal affairs of sovereign nations, this fevered hatred, combined with the increasing accessibility of cheap home kits for genetic engineering, chemical manufacture, and nanoparticle design, have made it essential for civilized nations to act. No longer can we tolerate individuals with bloodlust in their hearts and the means to create new, untold horrors in the privacy of their basements. How long do we have before one of these twisted, damaged souls unleashes a holocaust on this earth, one from which we cannot recover?

It is our duty to help these people, to bring them in from the cold. If their own governments won't help them, then we will.

Thank you. If you have questions, I'd be glad to answer them now.

Chairwoman: Thank you, Colonel Wright, for your testimony. As you know, we are on a short clock here this morning, so I think we should just jump right into questions. Let me begin by commending you on this important public service and your efforts to keep our nation safe. To put it bluntly, we are running out of time. The advancements in biology, chemistry, and nano-manufacturing over the last 2 decades have put the power to destroy civilization in the hands of people who cannot control themselves and hold only contempt for the rest of the world. Senator Wilkes?

Senator Wilkes: Thank you Ms. Chairwoman. Colonel Wright, what you are proposing is altering the minds of people you don't like against their will. How do you square this mission with the medical oath you took to "do no harm?"

Colonel Wright: These are people who already don't have a choice. Their governments are indoctrinating and drugging their children. Their economies are in collapse. They need our help.

Senator Wilkes: Colonel, the road to hell is paved with good intentions. Are we so arrogant as to believe our way is the right way?

Colonel Wright: If by "our way" you mean the approach adopted by leaders of both parties in closed session and by the UN and our allies, then yes, we do believe "our way" is the right way. "Our way" is the way of peace and cooperation. It is the path towards making positive contributions to society.

Senator Wilkes: Yes, yes, peace and cooperation. Sounds very nice until it is your mind that is being altered. Doesn't this all sound a little Orwellian to you?

Colonel Wright: I admit the third step makes most people uneasy, but the techniques have been proven safe with our very own children, they have passed through numerous trials and commissions. And remember, all the models show we are facing an existential threat here. The question is not "if" an individual or nation unleashes an attack on all mankind, but "when."

Chairman: Excuse me, Colonel, that buzzer is our final call for the floor vote on the confirmation of the new Director of National Security. Clearly, that's an important interruption. Colonel, we will continue this another time. This meeting is adjourned.

2060

Impact on Scenario 8: A Warm Reception.

In the original scenario, we focused on the challenge of developing international consensus for action on the issue of global climate and the possibility of unintended adverse consequences. In this update to the scenario, we see a world where global climate change has been mitigated in part by effective interagency teamwork and diplomacy.

Special Envoy and Green Earth Team Lead Amanda Huygens stepped out on the balcony of the U.S. Embassy in New Delhi. The reception was in full swing inside and she needed to catch a breath of fresh air. As dusk gathered, she looked wistfully over the city towards the India Gate. Through the closed French doors, she could hear the string quartet playing her favorite Strauss waltz as the festivities continued without her.

Decades of hard work from her and her interagency team had paid off. Planetary carbon dioxide levels had dropped off to pre-1970s levels; temperatures were back to and stabilized at pre-industrial levels. While some countries grumbled that the world was now too cold and that the lower temperatures were degrading their agricultural sectors, the consensus was a sigh of relief.

New nanotechnological materials had been the key. They enabled cleaner, more efficient, and distributed power, supporting a new hydrogen and solar economy. When the price for hydrogen power dropped below the price of fossil fuels without subsidy, the entire world seemed to shift overnight.

Amanda and her team worked both domestically and internationally to develop the new technologies and smooth the transition to hydrogen power. She negotiated reductions with the oil rich countries. Russia and Saudi Arabia were the last to give up on fuel oil and did so only when they were shown that they were losing money.

The lower average temperatures were a victory, but the real celebration was over the fact that the world had met the challenge of global climate change and maintained economic growth at the same time. Instead of locking the world into an austere version of the 1960s, Amanda and her team had focused their attention on win-win opportunities, allowing the underdeveloped world to develop and release greenhouse gases until remediation technologies could be put in place.

In 2060, the world was richer and cleaner than it had ever been. The only "underdeveloped" countries left in the world were those led by autarkic dictators and thugs. They were too few and far between to affect the climate on their own.

"I guess I've got to get a new job," Amanda whispered to herself.

"That may be wishful thinking," chimed Marta, her "automated personal access liaison" or aPAL. "The Earth's magnetosphere appears to be weakening."

"Marta, you're such a downer," thought Amanda.

"Excuse me, Amanda. The Canadian Ambassador has arrived for your party and has requested to see you," interrupted Marta.

Ambassador, welcome to the Embassy. Enjoy the refreshments. I'll be with you shortly, thought Amanda as she turned back to the party.

Impact on Scenario 9: It's a Small World.

In the original scenario, we explored the implications of a very different future, wherein small, molecular scale machines (nanotechnology robots or "nanobots") had become ubiquitous. In this updated scenario, the Director of National Security has created a standing Nanotech Interagency Team to smooth the transition to a nanotech world.

In 2037, the age of nanotech could have come to a screeching halt when unmoderated, self-replicating nanobots escaped accidentally from a design plant on the outskirts of Mexico City.

The so-called "gray goo" would have expanded from the plant in an ever increasing arc of destruction had the U.S. Nanotech Fast Response Team not been established in 2011. Over the following decades, the N-Fast Team had trained local first responders and industry around the world in effective techniques and tools for combating runaway nanobots. N-Fast also provided safety guidelines and certifications that most countries, including Mexico, had adopted. The result was that the Mexico City leak had been detected almost as soon as it occurred. It was rapidly contained and neutralized and only made page A-12 of the *New York Times* and *Gazette* feed.

Miranda Chavez, the U.S. Chief Nanotech Officer and head of the interagency N-Fast Team smiled with pride when she stumbled across the old electronic clipping. She had been only a junior member of the National Security Professional Corps at the time, but the N-Fast Team had been her first assignment. It was exciting in those days, because everything was so new and changing so rapidly. It really was a different time.

Over the next 20 years, nanotech had transformed the world in ways too numerous to count, and N-Fast had been there to ease the path forward. In conjunction with the National Assessment and Visioning Center, it monitored and extrapolated emerging technology trends and designed policy pathways that would foster the technologies without sacrificing safety and the environment.

Working with the International League of Democracies and the UN, N-Fast and the State Department negotiated a series of treaties determining how the world's resources would be managed and how to avoid conflict in the future. Together they establish a "blue goo" nanobot force to enforce international law in the sea, air, and beneath the earth's surface.

Within this framework, ever more sophisticated nanotech spread throughout the world with minimal impact on the environment and without the threat of warfare. The efficiencies of nanotechnology had brought the cost of most goods down below the former price of the constituent raw materials. Nano production required significantly less energy than traditional macroscopic production and resulted in no appreciable waste. The need for transportation was also largely eliminated by the ability to make products just about anywhere.

The world grew richer and healthier by leaps and bounds. The world of 2060 was a world without hunger, poverty, disease, and aging.

Beginning in the 2040s, N-Fast, through a consortium of industrial and religious organizations, had taken a leading role in providing free nano assemblers worldwide to produce the most basic human necessities. Simultaneously, global competition ensured the spread of more sophisticated nano production facilities worldwide, making even luxury goods available for a song. Nano businesses primarily made their money through creating new and more fashionable products. Older designs were quickly copied and made available for free to anyone on the mesh network.

Real estate was the only remaining high priced good, and even that was changing now as the nano industry honed its ability to design and "grow" new land out of the sea floor and in less hospitable regions of the world. Deserts and tundra alike were becoming paradisaical oases, for the right price.

Miranda wondered if the nanotech revolution would turn to space next. She wondered what the future would hold.

CHAPTER 5

A DEFENSE INDUSTRIAL BASE SCENARIO

Sheila R. Ronis

INTRODUCTION

Future scenarios such as this are designed to unlock the mind from its preconceptions in the hope of revealing undiscovered insights. This process can make some futures that have heretofore more or less been taken for granted appear less plausible, and prepare decisionmakers to look for signs of likewise unexpected futures. To repeat: the goal is not to predict the future. Rather, it is to think about the future and to be better prepared for it as the future unpredictably unfolds.

Weaknesses in our defense industrial base supply chain, dependency on third-party vendors, continual disregard for the Berry Amendment, and lack of foresight regarding the interplay between the global economy and national security are the root causes of failure in this scenario.

The task is to ensure that the vulnerabilities we highlight are never allowed to catch us by surprise or unprepared. This will require a shift from hindsight to foresight. Indeed, the necessary prerequisite for creating a better, safer national security environment for tomorrow starts with the ability to envision it. While drawing on lessons from history is certainly important, nowhere in the U.S. Government will one find personnel dedicated exclusively to developing overarching strategy with a long-term view. It is imperative to remedy this deficiency in order to avoid disastrous consequences, and reduce risks—both potential and real.

The 9-11 Commission Report concluded that the devastating attacks on September 11, 2001, were successfully executed due primarily to a failure of imagination on part of leaders who did not fully understand the gravity of the threat we faced. One of the most compelling aspects about the following case study is that although it takes place in the future, it relies very little on imagination. This scenario is not a product of fantasy or prediction but rather of practical reasoning and logical deduction. To be sure, the framework required for disaster in this scenario to unfold is largely already set.

CREATING AN OPPORTUNITY

During the course of the last 30 years, the Chinese have infiltrated critical elements of the U.S. industrial base, which is, of course, inseparable from the defense industrial base. In addition to targeting automotive, aerospace, and specialty metals, they have paid particular attention to the electronics industry. Through mergers, joint ventures, outright acquisition and industrial espionage, they have gained access to and control of sensitive technologies.

This is especially true in the area of electronic connectors, devices used to join electrical circuits, which are absolutely critical to every machine relying on electric using power. For reasons unknown to most of the world, the Chinese government designated these simple devices as a high priority sector, and by 2006 China was producing a third of the worlds' supply of electronic connectors.

Why? For the Chinese, motivation came after carefully scrutinizing U.S. Patent # 4972470 published November 20, 1990:

> A configurable connector between two or more devices with at least one of the devices being capable of programming the connector through an interface therewith. The connector contains programmable electronic circuitry capable of being instructed by the device whereby the connector assumes a desired connecting configuration and/or function. In one embodiment the connector is programmed to inquire and determine the configuration of the device to which it is connected. With the results of its analysis the connector adapts the necessary timing, pin-outs, voltages, and other parameters to assure proper communication between the connected devices. In other embodiments the connector contains electronic components to add specific functions for data exchange, such as data buffering, data encryption and the like. In addition, the connector is programmable with interchangeable pin designations thereby obviating the need for rewiring for different applications and physical connections.[1]

Moreover, a 2007 press release from ITT Electronic Components made clear the method and reason behind the Chinese quest for dominance in this area: the company had developed a variety of special-purpose electrical connectors designed for harsh environment and mission-critical applications in the military, aerospace, and hydrospace industries, including special release connectors, bulkhead and hull-penetrating connectors, and custom cable assemblies:

> ITT's special release connectors for aerospace applications feature special umbilical and lanyard release functions that automatically disconnect at the time of

system launch. These connectors can incorporate both pneumatic and electrical lines in the same assembly and are ideal for interstage separation, weapons storage and pylon applications.²

Special connector capabilities for harsh undersea applications include custom connectors for submarine sonar sets; wet mateable connectors, and umbilical cable assemblies for hull-mounted sonar arrays; lanyard-release connectors and umbilical cable assemblies for torpedo tube-launch missile systems; header assemblies for sonar system canisters; hull and missile tube penetrations; and a complete set for surface ship launch systems.

ITT's custom connectors and assemblies are specified in a number of major aerospace and hydrospace programs, including the Patriot and Tomahawk missiles, the Delta IV Launch Vehicle, the International Space Station, and the CVN-78 aircraft carrier scheduled to launch in 2015. The custom service includes rapid prototyping from ITT's comprehensive model shop and complete in-house testing at ITT's fully approved product evaluation lab.³

The Chinese realized they had stumbled onto just what they needed to defeat a technologically superior and network-centric U.S. military. Proceeding in an inconspicuous, seemingly harmless way, they have wasted no time acquiring this technology and begun taking the steps necessary to one day implement their insidious strategy.

They were able to take advantage of a lax security environment within the U.S. global supply and supplier chain, a favorable political climate thanks to massive investment capabilities and opportunities offered by Beijing, a rapidly eroding U.S. industrial base, and multiple states all too eager to restore jobs lost to outsourcing. Under the pretext of a benign investment, U.S.-based businesses—fronting for the Chinese firm Norinco—acquired a controlling interest in the company developing this "smart" electronic connector and imbued it with new capabilities, including distance programming. Research revealed Norinco was established under the guidance of the Communist Party's State Council in 1980, and is overseen by the Commission on Science, Technology and Industry for National Defense (COSTIND). According to the congressional testimony of Gary Milhollin of the Wisconsin Project on Nuclear Arms Control in 1997, Norinco subsidiaries in the United States include: Beta Chemical, Beta First, Beta Lighting, Beta Unitex, Larin, and others.[4]

China, recognizing that it could now totally infiltrate the U.S. industrial and military industrial base, it targeted four developing and ongoing weapons systems programs: The F-22 Raptor/F-35 Lightning II; Aegis fleet defense and countermeasures system; Bradley Fighting Vehicle; and the Advanced Amphibious Assault Vehicle (AAAV).

The efforts of the Chinese were made easier as the U.S. Department of Defense (DoD) continued to open the developmental architecture of their weapons systems and implemented an important series of mandates. The first of these was initiated by Secretary of Defense William Perry, who in 1991 announced the DoD *Strategic Acquisition Initiative* (SAI) which requires U.S. defense contractors to look first to COTS (Commercial Off-The-Shelf) products when developing new technology and upgrades. In 1994, Secretary Perry's memorandum *"Specs and Standards—A New Way of Doing Business"* mandated preference for commercial standards and products. Then, in 1997 Secretary of Defense William Cohen launched a *Defense Acquisition Reform Initiative,* which accelerated COTS.

These mandates required defense contractors, including Boeing, Lockheed-Martin, Northrop-Grumman, Raytheon, General Electric, General Dynamics Electric Boat Division, Pratt and Whitney, and others, to sow the seeds of operationally comprised weapons and propulsion systems. The rationale, with caveat, is as follows:

> The motivation for using COTS components is that they will reduce overall system development costs and involve less development time because the components can be bought instead of being developed from scratch. However, it comes with a significant side effect that the software component integration work and dependency on a third-party component vendor may incur significant additional cost.[5]

This could prove to be useful for software development because of the ever-increasing costs. Many considered COTS to be the Silver Bullet during the 1990s, but COTS development came with many not-so-obvious trade-offs (overall cost and development time can definitely be reduced, but often at the cost of an increase in software component integration work and dependency on a third-party component vendor).

According to the *Journal of Defense Software Engineering*, "Far from the promised panacea, the use of COTS components introduces new trade-offs and issues, especially with risk management, component integration, system reliability, and cost of sustainment."[6] And as the events of May 2015 will confirm, the concern over "dependency on a third-party component vendor" was all too true. The move towards globalization and the assumption that it is no longer necessary to protect and perpetuate the U.S. industrial base has led many in the DoD to assume that performance and cost-effectiveness are the only real criteria for ensuring that the U.S. warfighter gets the best equipment, and that where it comes from is irrelevant.

This atmosphere created by the COTS mandate within the U.S. supplier base also led many to ignore the Berry Amendment, which called for specialty metals critical to national security to be sourced only here. The nullification of "Buy American" requirements by the U.S. military, and the near destruction of the MILSPEC product identification and specifications code for military hardware and software components, would prove to have disastrous consequences.

These changes have caused some concerned individuals within industry, government, and the Pentagon to derisively call the changing state of affairs in terms of weapons systems development and procurement, along with acquisition of support materiel, "the Wal-Mart Military." Economy and competitiveness, not security and performance, are the overarching parameters of DoD supplier participation.

National security vulnerabilities are literally being built into our offensive, defensive, and detection systems. A veritable Pandora's box of systems security compromise was thrust open due to a gradual reduction in standards and shortsightedness by too many within industry and the government.

This is how weaknesses in our defense industrial base supply chain, dependency on third-party vendors, continual disregard for the Berry Amendment, and lack of foresight regarding the interplay between global economy and national security have set the stage for disaster. It is only a matter of when — not if — disaster will occur.

THE SCENARIO

The following scenario takes place 6 years into the future, in 2015. By 2011, China controlled 75 percent of the world's electronic connector production.

South China Sea: 0700 Zulu. 6 May 2015.

The U.S. Seventh Fleet, led by the carrier USS *George H.W. Bush* (CVN 77) has been deployed to send a strong message to China's totalitarian leaders who are amassing troops, aircraft, and vessels for what is apparently to be a full-scale assault against Taiwan. The People's Republic of China (PRC) is justifying this action in accordance with the anti-secession law passed by the National People's Congress on March 14, 2005, which created a legal framework for the use of force against Taiwan by declaring that China would "employ non-peaceful means and other necessary measures to protect China's sovereignty and territorial integrity."

Years of preparation for such an invasion make the U.S.-backed Taiwanese military a formidable foe, and it will not be overrun easily. Nevertheless, competence in matters military and strength of will cannot withstand China's parity in capability and equal strength of will, especially in combination with overwhelming numerical superiority within the People's Liberation Army (PLA), Air Force (PLAAF), Navy (PLAN), and air arm (PLANAF).

This disturbing reality is exactly why the U.S. Seventh Fleet was deployed the moment satellite ground imagery, growing communications traffic, and human intelligence determined an attack against Taiwan was inevitable.

Years of Preparation: Chinese Force Modernization.

In 2005, defense analyst Giuseppe Anzera outlined his view of a Chinese Navy in technological transition:

> Chinese shipyards have already completed two 052C-class ships, which are expected to be commissioned in 2005. It is probable that the PLAN intends to bring at least six ships of this class into service, deploying them in the three main operative battle groups that form the bulk of Beijing's fleet. This strengthening of forces will constitute a notable improvement in the performance of China's high sea forces.
>
> Deployment of this class is proceeding in parallel with the construction and acquisition of a number of new surface and submarine vessels. This emerging situation can suggest some foreign policy scenarios related to Beijing's moves in the next years.
>
> In regard to China's surface fleet (presently consisting of 64 large combatant units: 21 destroyers and 43 frigates), for the next decade Beijing will be committed to the demanding process of replacing obsolete ships, which had for so long reduced the Chinese Navy to a mere coastal fleet, with more modern units. For this reason, PLAN continues to bring into service units of Russian Sovremenny-class destroyers, while pursuing the construction of 052B and 052C-class warships, in addition to the construction of a completely new ship, being built in China's Dalian shipyard, that is expected to be very large and loaded with heavy surface armament (probably similar to Russia's Slava-class cruisers).
>
> At the moment, the creation of an extensive shipborne air force by building and deploying aircraft carriers does not seem to have priority in China. Beijing appears more interested in gaining time studying foreign equipment (as in the case of the aircraft carrier

Varyag, a former Soviet carrier initially acquired from Ukraine, which is badly deteriorated and only 70 percent completed in terms of becoming militarily operational) and then proceeding, in the future and without particular haste, to build its first domestically-built aircraft carrier.[7]

By 2009, China's plans for a blue water navy were confirmed with the admission by Defense Minister Liang Guanglie that the PLAN was seeking to build its first carriers. The Ukrainian-built *Varyag*, moreover, was refitted and returned to operational status in 2010 under the name *Shi Lang*. By 2014, two 50,000 to 70,000-ton carriers were completed 1 year ahead of schedule and joined the 67,500-ton *Shi Lang*, putting to rest the argument of several defense analysts that the Chinese were not interested in near-term development of a blue water force capable of slugging it out with powerful U.S. surface fleets deployed globally.

The force also includes enhanced Sovremenny-class destroyers equipped with new carrier-killing ship-to-ship missiles, super-quiet Victor III-based nuclear-powered and very quiet Kilo-class diesel-electric submarines, and 60-knot hydrofoil and catamaran littoral combat vessels, all equipped now with supersonic rocket torpedoes. The U.S. Navy recognized in 2005 the powerful threat represented by these Russian-developed weapon systems and has been working for the past 6 years on developing countermeasures. But even now, in 2015, China's current generation weapon called Shkval (Squall) is tough to defeat.

In a surprising twist, help to counter this threat came from Russian President Dmitri Medvedev who, shortly after his rise to power, realized in 2009 along with others in the Russian government and military, that their prolonged and profound technological and tactical assistance programs to Chinese weapons development had put Russia at risk. The years of joint exercises and the comfort level generated by ideological commonality were nothing more than a means to a very large end by the Chinese.

In short, Russia had been used. Consequently, Medvedev ordered the immediate development of Shkval countermeasures, and permission for the Americans and other Western partners to gain access to the technology. The solution came in the form of a submerged and surface-launched anti-rocket torpedo, which was aimed and launched completely independent of human interaction in a manner consistent with the Phalanx close-in anti-missile guns deployed by the fleet. The Russian system has been integrated into a common platform with the SSTDS torpedo defense system and AN/SLQ-28 NixieAS (anti-Shkval) torpedo countermeasures system, from Sensytech Inc. of Newington, Virginia.

The AN/SLQ-28 is deployed on all combat ships of the Seventh Fleet with the exception of the mine countermeasures and landing dock and submarine tenders. It works in concert with the Raytheon AN/SLQ-35 (V) electronic warfare system which detects hostile radar emissions using two sets of antennae, with the system analyzing the pulse repetition rate, the scan mode, the scan period, and the frequency. The system identifies the threat and its direction, produces a warning signal and interfaces with the ship's countermeasures systems, inclusive of the superb RIM-161(B) Aegis ballistic missile defense (BMD) utilizing the exo-atmospheric Raytheon SM-3 (standard missile) capable of short and medium range missile and intercontinental ballistic missile (ICBM) intercepts outside of the earth's atmosphere.

In 2004, according to reports, Russia, with Vladimir Putin's approval, had offered to sell the Taiwanese (through the United States) Kilo-class submarines with the ability to launch the quite lethal Sunburn and Yakhont anti-ship missiles in addition to Shkval rocket torpedoes. This, of course, was a very direct means for Taiwan to counter the threat of the Kilos of the same weapons capacity already in China's PLAN inventory, but there is no indication whether the deal was consummated.

In the skies, U.S. naval and air force aviators expect to encounter the Sukhoi SU-27-derived *Jiang* F-11 and the brand new *Shenyang* F-12 fighter aircraft designed to be operationally paired in a manner not dissimilar to the General Dynamics F-16 and the Boeing/McDonnell-Douglas F-15. The F-12 is similar in appearance to the F-22 *Raptor* and designed as an air superiority fighter melding technology — including an internal weapons bay and stealth — and tactics learned from interaction with Russian, Israeli, French, and U.S. aerospace sector contacts both overt and covert. It is said to be able to defeat the U.S. Navy's and Marine Corps F/A-18 *Super Hornet*, the USAF's F-15 and F-16, and effectively contend with F-22 and F-35 *Lightning II*. Force commanders are expecting initial engagement with fifth generation indigenously produced *Xian Jian Hong Flying Leopard* JH-7 fighter-bombers equipped with M variant YJ82(M) anti-ship missiles.

USAF B-2 *Spirit* stealth bombers newly modified to carry extra-long range (2,500 nm) anti-ship and hardened target destroying cruise missiles, have been deployed from the reactivated Wurtsmith Air Force Base in Oscoda, Michigan, to support the Seventh Fleet operations in the event the South China Sea engagement moves rapidly out of theater as a result of

China's transition to full war footing. It is hoped they will serve as a deterrent to this very real possibility.

B1-B *Lancers* operating out of Ramstein and establishing in-theater homes temporarily at bases in South Korea, Japan, and Taiwan, are equipped with Boeing AGM-84J Harpoon Block III anti-ship missiles. They have one mission: take out the Zhu Rongji should fleet saber rattling become active combat.

If the Americans, backed logistically by several NATO allies, only knew that the battle was lost before it ever began. In the ensuing confrontation, destruction was inflicted by unconventional means which rendered inconsequential the understanding of Chinese force capacity and our knowledge of weaponry sophistication.

THE BATTLE BEGINS

Radar Contact: Chinese Battle Group
0724 Zulu. 6 May 2015.

The Seventh Fleet Battle Group, led by the Nimitz-class USS *George H. W. Bush* and the theater level force command and control ship USS *Blue Ridge*, is supported by a strong mix of Ticonderoga and Oliver Hazard Perry-class Aegis guided missile cruisers including USS *Shiloh*, USS *Chancellorsville*, and USS *Rumsfeld*; Arleigh Burke-class guided missile destroyers like USS *Curtis Wilbur*; the amphibious assault ship USS *Essex* carrying advanced amphibious assault vehicles whose mission is to assault and temporarily neutralize the Hainan Island military base threat; the Avenger-class mine countermeasures ship USS *Guardian* and USS *Angel*; Los Angeles-class attack submarines USS *City of Corpus Christi, Detroit,* and *Houston*, and the brand new littoral combat ships USS *Freedom, Paul Revere, and Security*. The latter vessels were specifically designed and on station to contend with the PLAN's newly deployed Dragon-class hydrofoils and Laozi-class catamarans.

The U.S. battle strategy is one of total containment of the Chinese PLA, PLAN, PLANAF, and PLAAF on the sea, in the air, and on the ground. The Chinese Second Fleet Battle Group was led by the new 70,500 ton carrier *Zhu Rongji*, (modeled on the Kuznetsov-class carrier *Varyag*) and by most assessments the near-equal of the *Kitty Hawk* in speed, crew complement, attack/defense technological capability, and aircraft capacity (which happens to include the SU-30 MKK3, Yak-141 VTOL-inspired AV8 Harrier-type J-13 supersonic jump jet, naval variant J-12s, anti-submarine helos, and advanced turbo-prop airborne early warning (AEW) craft with eerie resemblances to the E-2C *Hawkeye* complemented by land-based Y-8 surveillance and electronic warfare and KJ-2000 AWACS aircraft). It is supported by a similar strong mix of 052B and 052C-class guided missile destroyers utilizing a clone of the Aegis detection system (acquired through a U.S. front company which managed to become a subcontractor to Lockheed-Martin) and anti-submarine variable depth sonar, three new Russian Slava-class derived guided missile cruisers built at the Dalian shipyards as was *Rongji*, and very high speed hydrofoil and catamaran configuration littoral combat ships.

Most worrisome to American commanders is that the Chinese carrier, cruisers, and destroyers are equipped with the positively lethal, virtually indefensible Russian Raduga Machine Building Design Bureau 3M-82 Moskit Sunburn (rated at Mach 2.5) and the near mach 3 NPO Mashinostroyeniva — P-800 Yakhont anti-ship missiles. When introduced in 2001, they were and are considered the most advanced cruise missiles in the world. The Navy also knew then that the Sunburn and Yakhont were designed to defeat both the Aegis anti-missile system and the Phalanx close-in point defense weapon through their ability to perform violent last second countermeasures lock avoidance maneuvers, typically designated rolling action. Consequently, there was immediate incentive to accelerate development and deployment of the Rolling Action Missile (RAM) defense system, yet unproven in combat.

With 75 miles of open sea now separating the opposing fleets, all hopes of a peaceful resolution are dashed as 12 JH-7s are picked up closing on the American fleet at high subsonic speed and 4,000 ft. altitude. They are known to be equipped with the YJ82M anti-ship missiles with at least 65-mile range.

F/A-18E/F *Super Hornets*, having replaced the F-14 *Tomcat* as the main fleet defense fighter after its retirement in 2006 and now joined by F-35 *Lightning IIs*, immediately engage the JH-7s before they reach minimum release point range and down five aircraft in short order. The Aegis 9.0 equipped destroyers *Cowpens* and *Curtis Wilbur* bring down another five, while the remaining two aircraft launch a spread of eight missiles. Yellow fireballs in the sky seconds after launch are all that are left of the Chinese aircraft.

Now, the fleet must deal with eight missiles tracking both *George H. W. Bush* and *Blue Ridge*. *Cowpens* takes out four Aegis tracked YJ82Ms while *Shiloh* destroys another two. *George H. W. Bush's* Phalanx 30mm close-in ship defense weapons featuring depleted uranium rounds and Battlespace Adaptive Artificial Intelligence (BAAI, commonly known as "BAA-BAA tech"), must deal with the last two, and they do.

The American Fleet Responds.
0745 Zulu. 6 May 2015.

The American fleet, having successfully fended off the Chinese air attack, is now preparing its own. By all analyses, the superior training of U.S. naval, air, and ground forces—the latter having already been deployed at strategic access points along the Chinese shoreline and borders via amphibious attack vessels and Boeing C17C *Globemaster IIIs* at forward areas—was expected to carry the day.

In parallel with the air and naval operations, fast and agile, well-positioned, rapid deployment forces consisting of U.S. Army and Marine Special Forces were supported by Bradley and Stryker armored fighting vehicles with advanced target acquisition and engagement systems in addition to newly developed reactive armor and anti-tank missile countermeasures. The lessons learned in Iraq during intense counterinsurgency operations resulted in a DoD directive to BAE Systems to launch an accelerated program to ensure prolonged survivability of the Bradley—and concomitantly, the Stryker—in high threat arenas.

They had specific instructions to secure and neutralize key Chinese installations, military and infrastructural, on Hainan Island in this case, via a fast attack strategy dictating they spend no more time in the target area than was absolutely necessary: The technology gap in weapons had been reduced significantly over the last 2 decades, and they had no intention of taking on the full might of the Chinese ground forces with their overwhelming numerical superiority in both men and equipment.

Nevertheless, network-centric warfare had absolutely come into its own with comprehensive real-time data linking and program actuation between U.S. forces deployed, all taking advantage of Satellite Internet (SATNET), an expansion of Voice Over Internet Protocol (VoIP) telecommunications. As crowded as low earth orbital spaceways had been in 2008, it was even more so in 2015, with a complex array of communications, global positioning systems (GPS), and terrestrial surveillance satellites from several nations. Ominously, even the "bad actor" nations like Iran, North Korea, and now, thanks to China's aggressive space program, even Cuba and Venezuela had eyes in the sky.

Soon this system would compound a significant vulnerability of American forces. With aircraft target acquisition, tracking, and firing solutions data only seconds away, the force commander on *George H. W. Bush* gave the order to counterattack, using a coordinated anti-ship missile launch. But that attack never materialized. As if by magic, radar screens went blank; Aegis real-time/symbiotic detection and attack electronics suite missile launch data disappeared from the ship and system linked aircraft. A new, devastating reality instantly set in: information flow had stopped completely. Even worse, all defensive and offensive capabilities, much of it Aegis-based, were neutralized.

A scenario of chaos and confusion rapidly emerged for the Seventh Fleet and all support forces. Ship commanders suddenly found themselves unable to control their vessels as new commands, source unknown, were fed into GPS-based navigation systems.

When *Shiloh* realized it was on a collision course with *Cowpens* at 32 knots, IT officers and other shipboard computer/telecommunications specialists tried vainly to disable the system and invoke manual override. They were unsuccessful. The *Shiloh* ripped *Cow-*

pens in two and, in so doing, tore a gaping hole in her own bow. Both ships sank in minutes.

Officers and technicians aboard the command and control vessel *Blue Ridge* were astonished to see firing solutions developed from combined Aegis, AWACs, and other offensive/defensive weapons and countermeasures systems data appearing on screen and being simultaneously uplinked to all ships, submarines, and aircraft. Their astonishment soon became devastation: *the new targets were all American*. The USS *Stethem*, another guided missile destroyer, had locked onto the frigate USS *Gary* and launched two Harpoon Block III supersonic anti-ship missiles at virtually point blank range, just sufficient for arming. *Gary* never had a chance, disappearing in a blinding flash and boiling sea.

In the skies overhead, 15 F-22 *Raptor* pilots approaching the battle arena at 47,000 ft in supercruise (Mach 1.5) were confident up to this point that their skyspace was incontestable, even though long range radar reveals up to 36 PLAAF and PLANAF aircraft ahead. Suddenly, they find they are unable to advance or reduce throttle settings, utilize RADAR, or arm weapons. Moreover, it appears the enemy aircraft have no problem tracking them. The fact is, not only are they sitting ducks, but they have no control over their aircraft. In what seemed a slow, yet awful ballet, one *Raptor* after another plunges into the sea or ground at supersonic speed, pilots unable to eject. Those that do not disintegrate in terrain impact are simply blown out of the sky by Chinese air-to-air missiles.

The F-35B *Lightning IIs*, having launched from the *George H. W. Bush* in their first offensive deployment after handover to the Navy in January 2011, are not faring any better, as the pilots vainly try to bring vectored thrust nozzles gone astray under some semblance of control. The aircraft are thus subjected to extreme super-maneuver g stresses and experience structural failure mid-air.

The undersea situation is every bit as dire. The captains of *City of Corpus Christi, Detroit,* and *Houston,* aware of the carnage on the surface, try to prevent launches of Tomahawk II cruise missiles that have been mysteriously reprogrammed to strike Taipei and Japan's Sasebo Naval Base, home of the Seventh Fleet. At the same time, they are desperate to prevent the Raytheon MK52 very high speed (150kt) torpedoes from launching against themselves. Weapons systems specialists and computer programmers are trying to stop the alien data feeds while working to restore some sensory capability. They need to know their status *now*—where, how fast, how deep—and if they are being tracked.

It is indeed the nightmare of nightmares for submariners, and unfortunately for *Houston, City of Corpus Christi* cannot prevent a torpedo launch which immediately acquires and attacks her. At 450-foot depth, the results are devastating as *Houston* breaks apart, and her death is heard with horrific clarity by the crews of her sister subs. *City of Corpus Christi* and *Detroit* will live to fight another day, but only because in desperation, her telecommunications and computer technicians have decided to do the equivalent of a system wide data wipe and then deenergize all systems, switching over to redundant, though minimal, control and sensing.

On the surface, as bad as it is, the worst is yet to come as the remaining ships of the Seventh Fleet, with no offensive/defensive capability other than manual control Phalanx and primary guns of the littoral combat ships and frigates, can only watch in stunned silence as the skies become filled with Sunburn and Yakhont anti-ship missiles launched at 50 miles distance by the Chinese Second Fleet. The waters of the South China Sea are infested with odd-looking wakes generated by surface and submarine launched long-range VA-111C Shkval rocket torpedoes.

The *George H. W. Bush* is hit by no less than six Yakhont nuclear-tipped missiles and simply disintegrates; *Blue Ridge* has no time to contemplate the destruction of the carrier as she is hit by a Sunburn with a 750 lb warhead, which tears a hole large enough to ensure her demise. In what is most certainly overkill, two rocket torpedoes hit her at supersonic speed, lifting her out of the water and simultaneously breaking the ship apart. The two pieces settle and sink with appalling rapidity. Only those crew members blown over the side during the missile and torpedo strikes survive.

Aftermath.
0803 Zulu. 6 May 2015.

Nothing remains of the surface Seventh Fleet save for the littoral combat ships *Freedom, Paul Revere*, and *Security*, whose 50kt capability and quick thinking technicians restored a measure of ship control and promptly took them out of the immediate battle space. All aircraft, save for the B-2s, which were ordered to turn away from the battle space by *Blue Ridge* when it became apparent that something had gone terribly wrong, have been destroyed either through control loss or Chinese air-to-air and surface-to-air missiles.

The land forces dispatched to secure installations on Hainan Island have been annihilated, their positions electronically compromised. Sixteen Bradley and Stryker fighting vehicles with their Marine and Special Forces complement, and the advanced amphibious assault vehicles (now known as expeditionary force vehicle, or EFV) launched from the *Essex*, were mysteriously immobilized. They had no chance against the strong force of Chinese WZ-11 attack helicopters, Type 97B infantry fighting vehicles, and Type 100A main battle tanks. Moreover, the AAAV mother ship *Essex* was hit by four rocket torpedoes, and seconds later, by a nuclear tipped Yakhont missile. In an instant, only debris and smoke were left where a ship had been. There were no survivors.

Future military historians would rank this U.S. naval force defeat—in terms of an upset—right alongside the Battle of Tsushima/Port Arthur during the Russo-Japanese War in 1905. Japanese forces, led by Admiral Togo, utterly defeated a numerically and technologically superior Russian battle group led by Admiral Rodzesvensky. This defeat had immediately changed the world's balance of power, with Japan emerging to replace Russia as a military and geo-political force to be reckoned with by the United States. On May 6, 2015, 110 years later, exactly the same thing had transpired here, with geo-political ramifications yet to be realized.

DESTRUCTION OF THE SEVENTH FLEET: THE CULPRIT

How and why did things go so terribly wrong? Through the use of distance programmable electronic connectors, the Chinese, using their Y-8C AEW and electronic intelligence (ELINT) aircraft, were able to activate imbedded programming in connectors within every system on ships, submarines, and aircraft of the

Seventh Fleet and vehicles of Fleet support forces. As noted in a *Chinese Defense Today* analysis in 2006:

> Like the U.S. C-130 Hercules, the Shaanxi Y-8 four-engine turboprop transport aircraft has been developed into many special purposes variants. The PLA Air Force was known to have been using the Y-8 for special electronic warfare (EW) missions including electronic intelligence (ELINT) and offensive electronic countermeasures (ECM) in the past, but little was known about these programs until an electronic warfare variant Y-8 was first spotted in operation in Summer 2004.[8]

While detailed information regarding the onboard mission equipment is not available, it is believed that the new EW/ELINT variant Y-8 is equipped with an extensive array of sophisticated intelligence gathering equipment to monitor enemy electronic activities. The aircraft may also be capable of launching offensive jamming against enemy communications and radar systems.

There has been a rumor suggesting that some of the mission equipment may come from the U.S. Navy EP-3 ELINT aircraft, which made an emergency landing in Hainan Island in April 2001 after colliding with a Chinese fighter, but this cannot be confirmed. The PLA may well be capable of developing its own indigenous EW/ELINT system as a result of the country's booming electronics and telecommunications industry.

The fact that Chinese manufacturers were able to provide a multitude of components at the tier 4 and below supplier level (at present, there is no requirement by the DoD to identify supplier origins beyond the third tier) for at least four critical weapons systems—the Aegis 9.0, the Bradley Fighting Vehicle, the F-22 Raptor/F-35 Lightning II, and the Advanced Amphibious Assault Vehicle, plus their control of electronic connector production, allowed an all but complete infiltration of the U.S. industrial and military industrial supply base. This same infiltration was made even easier when it was realized that virtually all ocean-borne shipping that was servicing the industrial base supply chain was in the hands of the Chinese. This provided multiple opportunities to control or deny movement of components and permitted the Chinese to disrupt the supply chain at will.

Epilogue.
0900 Zulu. 6 May 2015.

Every means by which the Americans can attack or defend has been neutralized, in a de facto sense, on a global scale. Committing the other carrier battle groups with their Nimitz-class carriers is out of the question, considering the utter destruction of the Seventh Fleet. The Chinese, sensing that they should seize the opportunity to become the dominant world power, decide to bring their ICBM force on line, with all large American cities and key bases targeted. Their ballistic missile program reached operational status 5 years sooner than Western intelligence sources had indicated, thanks to Boeing booster technology inadvertently provided in the late 1990s.

Now in full launch mode, the Chinese government is demanding that the United States sue for peace immediately or suffer the consequences, and the U.S. President, for a moment feeling he has no choice, takes steps towards the process of acceding to Chinese demands rather than risk a third global war wherein assured destruction was not mutual. Without warning, however, Chinese ICBMs sitting in their silos or sea-launch ships disguised as freighters, start exploding.

The Chinese Second Fleet, flush with victory over the Americans, has far less time to celebrate than imagined as its radars pick up incoming sea-skimming Harpoon Block IV long range (2500nm) supersonic anti-ship cruise missiles co-developed with the Russians. They had been launched from the American B-2s that had reversed course undetected after being ordered out of the battlespace by *Blue Ridge* before its destruction. Recognizing that the ships, submarines, and aircraft of the Seventh Fleet were somehow having their defensive/offensive and detection systems reprogrammed from a distant source, the B-2s linked with radar and communications-jamming EF-22 *Wild Ferrets*, whose performance surpassed that of the venerable EA-6D *Prowlers*, EF-111E *Ravens* and RC-135G *Rivet Joints* being phased out by the Air Force and Navy.

Thanks to temporary suppression of Chinese radars and communications, both airborne and surface, each of the 10 B-2s was able to select and engage multiple naval targets, with the *Zhu Rongji* disintegrating subsequent to the impact of seven air-launched Harpoon IVs. The carrier force was rapidly destroyed, save for two hydrofoil and one catamaran fast attack craft.

Miles above the battle zone, Chinese F-12s and SU-MKK3s find themselves under attack from an unseen foe as multiple aircraft are destroyed. Unknown to the Chinese and the rest of the world, work had continued on the hypersonic Lockheed-Martin SR-73 *Aurora*, and, unlike its predecessor the SR-71, an attack version A-14 had been developed and deployed.

Based in classified locations, 10 A-14s had been rushed—an expression taking on new meaning when an aircraft flies hypersonically—to the battle space when it became apparent the Seventh Fleet was in serious trouble. Flying at 100,000 ft and at Mach 6+, they tracked the Chinese fighters with enhanced look down-shoot down target acquisition radar.

In parallel actions, Chinese ICBMs were being destroyed in their silos and mobile launch platforms across China by heretofore unacknowledged (and undetected) Northrop-Grumman B-3 *Ghost* hypersonic transatmospheric future attack bombers. What became clear to the Chinese is that the A-14 and B-3 were impervious to distance reprogramming of vital systems, and, worse, could not be tracked.

Savvy Pentagon officials working with intelligence officers within the Central Intelligence Agency (CIA) and the National Security Agency (NSA), who since 9/11 had restructured intelligence services data-sharing platforms in accordance with the Patriot Act (Hart-Rudman recommendations as well) had worked to keep the development and production of the SR-73, A-14, and B-3 separate from an industrial base supply chain they felt was severely compromised. They knew the Berry Amendment was routinely ignored or skirted in regard to provision of defense specialty metals, and felt that open architecture and COTS mandates were creating a weapon systems performance and security disaster.

Northrop-Grumman, Lockheed-Martin, and Boeing IDS officials, under a special confidentiality arrangement, fully cooperated. Funding had already been allocated through the B-2 program, as some had suspected, not long after this super-secret project had been revealed. They named it Project Purity, and in the aftermath of the Seventh Fleet disaster Congress directed that all future critical weapon systems development and production programs would follow its strict guidelines calling for ALL supplier identification, a "homegrown" requirement (the UK, Canadian, and Australian defense firms were exempted) along with a strengthening of the Berry Amendment.

It was the Chinese who were suing for peace following the very timely intervention of the A-14, SR-73, and B-3. The Seventh Fleet had not died in vain.

ROOT CAUSES OF FAILURE

We have presented a future scenario that, under the current state of the industrial and military industrial base and its supply chain, can become all too real. We have documented the prime and subcontractors to the fourth tier, but beyond that it is next to impossible to develop additional supplier identification data. The DoD itself does not require component origins identification beyond the third tier, and this makes maintaining cohesion and program security within the manufacturing and supply base problematic.

The elements of national power that are not being managed effectively and/or integrated in this scenario are both military and economic. The major players include the Departments of State, Defense, Commerce, Treasury, Transportation, and the interagency Committee for Foreign Investment in the United States (CFIUS) process. All these departments, as well as Congress, have a say in how and where our weapon systems should be manufactured and how their supply chains should be managed, but nobody monitors it well enough or pays attention to issues like "electronic connectors" because they are considered commodities. The problem is complex, and since no one is responsible for the "big picture," no one is positioned to identify dangerous patterns as they emerge. In addition, high-impact, low-probability contingencies are of little interest to busy politicians who have no immediate incentive to express concern or initiate change. As a result, disasters like the one we describe in the scenario can arise.

One example of the government failing to act with an overarching strategy and failing to integrate existing elements of the national security policy decision-making apparatus is demonstrated by the CFIUS. The Committee on Foreign Investment in the United States is an interagency committee that serves the President in overseeing the national security implications of foreign investment in the economy. Since it was established by an Executive Order of President Ford in 1975, the committee has operated in relative obscurity, but in 2005 public and congressional concerns about the proposed purchase of commercial port operations in six U.S. ports by Dubai Ports World (DP World) sparked a firestorm of criticism and congressional activity during the 109th Congress concerning CFIUS and the manner in which it operates.

Owing to the attention caused by DP World, some Members of the 109th and 110th Congresses have questioned the ability of Congress to exercise its oversight responsibilities given the general view that CFIUS operations lack transparency. Other Members revisited concerns about the linkage between national security and the role of foreign investment in the U.S. economy. The DP World transaction also revealed that "the September 11, 2001, terrorist attacks may have fundamentally altered the viewpoint of some members of Congress regarding the role of foreign investment in the economy and the impact of such investment on the national security framework. These observers argue that this change requires a reassessment of the role of foreign investment in the economy and of the implications of corporate ownership of activities that fall under the rubric of "critical infrastructure."

> As a result, Congress amended the CFIUS process to enhance Congress's oversight role while it reduced somewhat the discretion of CFIUS to review and investigate foreign investment transactions in order to have CFIUS investigate a larger number of foreign investment cases. In addition, the DP World transaction has focused attention on long-unresolved issues concerning the role of foreign investment in the nation's overall security framework and the methods that are being used to assess the impact of foreign investment on the nation's defense industrial base and homeland security.[9]

In the 1st session of the 110th Congress, members approved measures that will amend the CFIUS process to provide greater oversight by Congress and increased reporting by the Committee on its decisions. In addition, the measures broaden the definition of national security and require greater scrutiny by CFIUS of certain types of foreign direct investments. The amendment process revealed significant differences between Congress and the administration over the operations of CFIUS and over the objectives the Committee should be pursuing. Most importantly for our study, it demonstrated that neither Congress nor the administration has been able thus far to define clearly the national security implications of foreign direct investment. This issue likely reflects differing assessments of the economic impact of foreign investment on the U.S. economy and differing political and philosophical convictions among members and between the Congress and the Administration.

We also know from interactions with Chinese representatives, industry spokesman, and government and military personnel that specific strategies are in place to gain control of various elements of the U.S. industrial and defense industrial bases. Colleagues in industry who have interacted with these same personnel have stated, "The acquisition budget for automotive, aerospace, textile (what's left of it), metal, energy, electronics, and telecommunications companies approaches one trillion dollars."[10] We have also been advised that a specific directive has been issued to find and secure any automotive suppliers with high technology capabilities that are in distress. The need for this strategy was demonstrated by the Chinese acquisition of the MG Rover Group (the last domestically owned mass-production car manufacturer in the British motor industry) when, subsequent to acquiring controlling interest, the Chinese wasted no time moving critical manufacturing elements and processes to China. An empty shell of a firm was left, along with a direct job loss of 5,000 personnel. China will now build the Rover 75 in China, Oklahoma, and other locales.

Regarding electronics firms, we have observed multiple instances wherein the approach of the Chinese has been a "helpful" offer of financial assistance for companies "until they worked their problems out." All that was required was for one or several of their personnel, depending on the size of the company, to come aboard as staff, "so they could better understand the inner workings of the company." This process has allowed the Chinese to undermine anti-industrial espionage, intellectual property, and proprietary and copyright laws by quite legitimately requesting a "sharing" of technological processes with "company colleagues" even though these colleagues were in a facility in Shandong province or Shanghai, for example.

According to U.S. intelligence officials, this is the means by which Aegis weapon system technology was stolen: a company fronting for the Chinese became a subcontractor to Lockheed-Martin during Aegis development and acquired enough data to construct its own clone. At this time, up to four Luyang II-class destroyers have been acknowledged as featuring this missile defense system.

CONCLUSION

The research that went into this analysis provided many lessons, including the following:
- If the United States is exporting large quantities of critical technologies to China, the Chinese will also most certainly benefit from them for military purposes.
- If American companies cannot provide transparency in their global supply chains, then they cannot answer the question, "Which components of our weapon systems are made outside of the United States?" The DoD must ask this question if it expects industry to provide answers below Tier III.
- As China becomes the manufacturing capital of the world, it will become increasingly difficult for all industries to comply with the Berry Amendment.
- If the Chinese control global shipping, they will not permit those ships to feed our economy or our military if we are at war with them. Even minor supply disruptions could produce eco-

nomic chaos in the United States and its surge capability would disappear.
- Congress needs to require DoD to resolve these problems, particularly how the first part of the scenario in which China's use of information and technological warfare to defeat U.S. forces will be prevented.
- If science, engineering, and technology skill sets are eroding within the United States across the board, it will not be long before we cannot compete economically or militarily with a China that out-produces us in scientists and engineers, in research and development (R&D), and in manufacturing capabilities and volumes. Congress needs to increase R&D for the sciences and engineering across the board. It should also find incentives and provide financial aid for young Americans who want to become scientists, engineers, diplomats, and linguists, skills the nation desperately needs.
- The United States needs a plan to "win" the war, economically, diplomatically, politically, and militarily with China and other emerging powers. Congress must task some U.S. Government entity to write this master plan for the nation.

The purpose of this scenario has not been to convince the reader that information and technological warfare with China is inevitable. Indeed, the threats that will emerge in the future are likely beyond our current contemplations. But one has to remember that it was not raining when Noah built the ark. It would be a mistake to limit our ideas about the future by the narrow experiences of our past. The goal of this case study, as with most historical case studies, is to expose flaws and weaknesses within the national security apparatus. Here, with the advantage of historical hindsight, this study calls attention to potential dangers of leaving current weaknesses in our defense industrial base and global supply chain unattended to. It articulates the importance of evaluating assumptions and questioning the meaning of events as they unfold.

While it can be dangerous to hold rigid beliefs about what tomorrow will bring, preparedness requires seeing possibilities before they become obvious. The value of a scenario like this lies not in the effort to solve the hypothetical problems of some distant tomorrow, but about making wise decisions today.

ENDNOTES - CHAPTER 5

1. U.S. Patent #4972370, Published November 20, 1990.

2. ITT press release, "Custom Connector and Special Products Program Shortens Product Development Time," January 1, 2007.

3. *Ibid.*

4. Gary Milhollin, Prepared testimony before Senate Governmental Affairs Subcommittee on International Security, Proliferation and Federal Services, Washington, DC, April 10, 1997.

5. Henry H. Liu, *Software Performance and Scalability: A Quantitative Approach*, Hoboken, NJ: John Wiley & Sons, Inc., 2009, p. 61.

6. Lieutenant Colonel Joe Jarzombek, "The Double-Edged COTS IT Sword," *CROSSTALK: The Journal of Defense Software Engineering*, No. 228-M, April 1998, p. 2.

7. "The Modernization of the Chinese Navy," *2005 Power and Interest News Report* (PINR), available from www.pinr.com.

8. *China Defense Today*, December 4, 2005.

9. Congressional Research Service Report, *The Committee on Foreign Investment in the United States (CFIUS),* James K. Jackson, Specialist in International Trade and Finance, February 4, 2010.

10. Myron D. Stokes, personal discussions with Dr. Sheila R. Ronis, 2007.

CHAPTER 6

NUCLEAR BOMB CASE STUDY

Lindsey Gehrig
Lauren Bateman
Sheila R. Ronis

METHODOLOGY

Methodologies for visioning use many different tools. Sometimes it is easier to learn lessons from a situation by reading a future history as described in the preceding chapter. In the present case study, analysis and synthesis tools were used to approach a very different scenario. Both methods are examples of the myriad tools available for learning and developing infrastructure to support the national security system.

INTRODUCTION

There is a bipartisan consensus in the government and among national security experts that a nuclear weapon in the hands of terrorists constitutes one of the gravest and most urgent threats currently facing the United States, a fact recognized in the national security strategy:

> Nuclear weapons are unique in their capacity to inflict instand loss of life on a massive scale. For this reason, nuclear weapons hold special appeal to rogue states and terrorists.[1]

Although the Federal Government has detailed plans for responding to a variety of homeland emergencies, a strategy detailing how federal agencies would respond to a nuclear attack does not yet exist. In addition, because federal efforts to protect against a nuclear attack are spread among multiple agencies, "determining the full range of existing efforts, coordinating the outcomes of these efforts, identifying any overlaps and gaps between them, and developing an architecture integrating current and future efforts" are necessary.[2]

In an effort to assess the degree to which the United States has an effective strategy to prevent and respond to a nuclear attack, the Project on National Security Reform asks four primary questions:

1. Did the U.S. Government generally act in an ad hoc manner or did it develop effective strategies to integrate its national security resources? The Department of Homeland Security's National Response Framework details how the United States plans to respond to a variety of emergencies, ranging from small incidents to the largest possible catastrophes. However, a strategy detailing how federal agencies, in cooperation with local and state governments, should respond to a nuclear attack does not yet exist.

2. How well did the agencies/departments work together to implement these ad hoc or integrated strategies? Because there is not a comprehensive response plan tailored specifically to a nuclear attack, lead agency responsibilities in the event of such a disaster remain undefined and unclear. In an effort to improve the coherence of interagency efforts, "the Bush administration . . . assigned various players to take the lead in coordinating interagency activities."[3] However, this effort has not achieved its intended goal and instead has resulted in "a confusing tangle of lead agency responsibilities that complicate rather than unify plan-

ning and resource allocation and are bound to sow confusion during emergency operations."[4]

3. What variables explain the strengths and weaknesses of the response? It is impossible to evaluate the strengths and weakness of the U.S. response to a nuclear attack because fortunately one has never occurred. Experts fear that, should a nuclear attack occur tomorrow, the following variables would contribute to a less than optimal response:

- Varying levels of interest and support for interagency cooperation by federal departments and agencies;
- Fragmentation of responsibilities and capabilities within the federal structure;
- The lack of primary agency responsibility and accountability;
- Inadequate strategic guidance from the federal level about the definition and objectives of preparedness and how states and localities will be evaluated in meeting those objectives;[5]
- Inadequate education, training, and equipment for emergency responders at the local, state and federal levels;[6]
- The lack of a well-defined process for two-way information-sharing between federal and state officials regarding strategic decisionmaking;[7]
- The absence of a sustained personal effort by the administration to take a central role in urging and overseeing the execution of interagency coordination efforts.[8]

4. What diplomatic, financial, and other effects and costs would result from these successes and failures? If the United States does not have a more specific and comprehensive strategy to respond to a nuclear attack,

not only will there be enormous initial devastation, but thousands of additional lives will be lost, billions of dollars will spent, and widespread unnecessary panic will ensue.[9]

This case is divided into four parts:
- Part I overviews the responsibilities of federal agencies as they are currently designated, which illustrates the great range of agencies involved in countering nuclear terrorism as well as the overlap in roles between agencies that currently causes ambiguity;
- Part II explains and evaluates the current strategies for preventing a nuclear attack;
- Part III explains and evaluates the various components involved in responding to a nuclear attack; and
- Part IV answers the four primary questions posed above that are central to the Project on National Security Reform.

PART I: OVERVIEW OF CURRENT AGENCY ROLES IN COUNTERING NUCLEAR TERRORISM

The following agencies are all an essential part of a multilayered defense strategy to protect the United States from a nuclear attack.

Department of Homeland Security.

One primary reason for establishing the Department of Homeland Security (DHS) in 2002 was to unite and coordinate the vast national network of organizations and institutions involved in efforts to secure the United States. The Secretary of Homeland Security is the principal federal official for domestic incident management. Since its inception, the DHS has generated pressure for the nation to take a national, interagency, intergovernmental perspective on emergency readiness and response. The problem, however, is that interagency planning requires a perspective different from the day-to-day focus of departments and agencies. For most, it is a secondary priority.

Department of Homeland Security: Domestic Nuclear Detection Office.

Residing within the DHS is the Domestic Nuclear Detection Office (DNDO), which is the lead agency for the detection of nuclear materials. Established on April 15, 2002, it was created "to enhance and coordinate federal, state, and local efforts to prevent radiological and nuclear attacks."[10] DNDO has two primary tasks: first, it is tasked with coordinating the nuclear detection efforts of federal, state, and local governments;[11] second, DNDO is "responsible for developing, acquiring, and deploying radiation detection equipment to support the efforts of DHS and other federal agencies."[12] DNDO was given statutory authority for these responsibilities by the SAFE Port Act of 2006.

To fully carry out DNDO's strategic objectives, close cooperation and coordination between the Departments of Homeland Security, Energy, Defense, and State, the Federal Bureau of Investigation, state and local governments, and the private sector are necessary. Many of these government organizations are jointly staffing the DNDO, and the DNDO coordinates and cooperates closely with other federal agencies when necessary.[13]

Department of Energy: National Nuclear Security Administration.

The Department of Energy (DOE), or more specifically, the National Nuclear Security Administration (NNSA), works to enhance national security through the military application of nuclear energy. The NNSA also maintains and enhances the safety, reliability, and performance of the U.S. nuclear weapons stockpile, including design, production, and testing, in order to meet national security requirements. As the nation's primary responder to any nuclear incident within the United States or abroad, the NNSA provides operational planning and training to counter domestic nuclear terrorism.[14] NNSA provides technical support to the DHS, Justice, State, and Defense in dealing with nuclear terrorism events and domestic nuclear weapon accidents and incidents.

The comprehensive list in Figure 6-1 sets forth the numerous federal agencies involved in preventing and responding to a nuclear attack. With dozens of actors at the federal level—not to mention those at the state, local, and tribal levels—sharing common national security objectives, coordination and oversight of the many disparate efforts remain a challenge.

TOOLS	FEDERAL DEPARTMENTS & AGENCIES
Prevention	
Secure nuclear warheads and materials in other countries	Department of Energy Department of Defense Department of State
Stabilize employment for nuclear personnel	Department of Energy Department of State
Reduce nuclear stockpiles worldwide	Department of Energy
Strengthen and enforce nonproliferation norms and regimes	Department of State
Improve economic conditions in foreign countries	Department of State USAID
Offense	
Locate and destroy terrorist training camps	Department of Defense Intelligence agencies
Identify and destroy nuclear processing facilities and storage sites	Department of Defense Intelligence agencies
Find and destroy terrorist networks	Intelligence agencies FBI and others
Defense	
Gather and analyze international intelligence	Intelligence agencies
Gather and analyze information on domestic threats	FBI and others
International law enforcement	Department of Homeland Security, others
Domestic law enforcement	FBI, others
Develop and install nuclear detection equipment at U.S. ports and international borders	Department of Energy Department of State
Train foreign police regarding nuclear smuggling	FBI Department of Defense
Customs, border security, and immigration	Department of Homeland Security Department of State
Protection of U.S. nonmilitary facilities	Department of Homeland Security Department of Energy
Protection of U.S. military bases	Department of Defense
Disaster preparedness	Department of Homeland Security Department of Health and Human Services Department of Energy
Attribution of source of nuclear materials or components	Department of Homeland Security
Response and Recovery	Department of Homeland Security Department of Defense Department of Health and Human Services

Figure 6-1. Agencies Involved in Countering Nuclear Terrorism.

Today, if the president asked at a cabinet meeting who is responsible for preventing nuclear terrorism, six or eight hands in the room might go up, or none. In conceiving, organizing, and orchestrating the elements of the government to focus on an absolute priority, someone must have lead responsibility and be held accountable.[15] Individually, no single department or agency is capable of providing 100 percent effectiveness in preventing or responding to a nuclear attack. A multiagency effort is appropriate and necessary, but the efforts of any single department are currently undercut by a lack of coherence and the absence of an overarching strategy. This will be further illustrated in the next two parts, which describe and evaluate the strengths and weaknesses of existing strategies for the prevention and response of a nuclear attack.

PART II: PREVENTING A NUCLEAR ATTACK ON THE UNITED STATES

The current U.S. strategy to prevent a nuclear attack involves three primary components: (1) securing existing materials; (2) preventing importation of fissile material; and (3) detecting and tracking the movement of fissile material worldwide. In addressing each of these elements, this report will first identify the current strategy and then evaluate the strengths and weaknesses of how this strategy is implemented.

International treaties (such as the Nuclear Nonproliferation Treaty [NPT]) and regulatory bodies (International Atomic Energy Agency [IAEA] and the Nuclear Suppliers Group [NSG]) are components of prevention which aim to prevent new states from developing nuclear weapon capabilities. Because these components of prevention are the topic of a separate PNSR case study, this report will focus on prevention from a weapons standpoint. This is of utmost concern because experts agree that "terrorists do not have the capability to go nuclear on their own since enriching uranium or reprocessing plutonium is beyond the reach of substate groups. They have to have help, witting or unwitting, from a government."[16] New nuclear states are clearly a grave threat to national and international security, but experts agree that it is far more likely that an attack will be traced to a government's existing inventory. The greatest current threat is from the vast stock of questionably secured nuclear materials in the former Soviet Union.[17]

Security and Accountability of Existing Materials.

Strategy. The best way to prevent a nuclear disaster is to deny terrorist organizations the opportunity to acquire the essential fissile materials. The mechanics of building a nuclear weapon represent a 60-year-old technology, and that knowledge is widespread, but as a simple matter of physics, without fissile material, there can be no nuclear explosion.[18] Therefore, the National Security Strategy of the United States consists of programs targeted at securing and accounting for both the existing nuclear stockpile of weapons and of raw fissile material.

There are hundreds of sources around the world from which terrorists could acquire an intact nuclear weapon or the fissile material to build one, but the most salient threat is from the poorly secured nuclear materials in Russia and other states in the former Soviet Union. The reason for this is not that these governments would knowingly sell nuclear materials, but simply because the former Soviet Union contains more nuclear weapons materials than any other country in the world and much of it is vulnerable to theft.[19] The current legislative framework to prevent the theft of nuclear materials from Russian stockpiles centers on the Nunn-Lugar Cooperative Threat Reduction programs (CTR). Costing nearly a billion dollars annually, these efforts and the projects they support have run for over a decade.[20] CTR programs, which were extended in 2007, work primarily with Russia and other former Soviet states to secure and destroy nuclear warheads and fissile materials, and to reemploy former Soviet weapons scientists.[21]

In addition to programs that concentrate on this region of the world, the broader strategy to secure and account for nuclear material worldwide focuses on: (1) keeping states from acquiring the capability to produce fissile material suitable for making nuclear weapons; and (2) deterring, interdicting, and preventing any transfer of that material from states that have this capability to rogue states or to terrorists.[22] As previously mentioned, a separate PNSR case study discusses part (I) of this strategy; this report will focus on part II.

Efforts to keep fissile material out of the hands of rogue states and terrorists focuses on the danger posed by inadequately safeguarded storage and manufacturing facilities. According to the current National Security Strategy, the Bush administration led a global effort to reduce and secure such materials "as quickly as possible" through several initiatives, including the Global Threat Reduction Initiative (GTRI), which expanded on the success of the CTR. In addition to locating, tracking, and reducing existing stockpiles of nuclear material, the GTRI also discourages the trafficking of nuclear material by placing detection equipment at key transport locations.[23]

Evaluation. The Cooperative Threat Reduction programs in Russia and the former Soviet Union are widely considered successful. They have accomplished the primary goal of helping Russia pay for the dismantling and securing of many deployed strategic weapons systems and related research, production, and storage facilities.[24] In addition, since 1992, more than 2,000 former Soviet intercontinental missiles have been dismantled and more than 7,200 nuclear warheads have been deactivated. Together, the United States and Russia have eliminated more nuclear weapons than the combined arsenals of Britain, France, and China.[25]

The success of these nuclear nonproliferation programs is largely attributed to three main factors: (1) that much of the responsibility for nonproliferation programs falls within the purview of a single director; (2) the strong, sustained leadership by senior directors who provide top-down guidance to resolve cross-agency and cross-program disputes; and (3) the attention focused on those programs by Congress and think tanks.[26]

Unfortunately, the coherence and effectiveness of the nonproliferation efforts are much less apparent in broader efforts to counter nuclear terrorism.[27] This has to do, in part, with what many experts feel is a disparity between strategic rhetoric and strategic action. For example, on the one hand, the National Security Strategy states that combating the threat of weapons of mass destruction (WMD) is a foremost priority and that "the Administration is leading a global effort to reduce and secure such materials as quickly as possible."[28] On the other hand, former U.S. Senator Sam Nunn, currently co-chair of the Nuclear Threat Initiative, warns that, "at the current pace, it will be several decades before this material is adequately secured or eliminated globally."[29]

Leaders across the U.S. political spectrum agree that nuclear weapons in the hands of terrorists constitute one of the most important threats the nation faces, but successfully countering that threat requires, among other things, additional funding and high-level political efforts to break the bureaucratic deadlock that prevents successful integration efforts among diverse federal departments and agencies.[30] The progress made by various nonproliferation programs serves as an example of how substantial, sustained efforts can lead to successful outcomes. Experts agree that an undertaking of this sort also needs to be implemented in broader efforts to counter nuclear terrorism.

Blocking Importation of Nuclear Materials into the United States.

Strategy. Long before the terrorist attacks of September 11, 2001 (9/11), the Federal Government has had in place a series of programs focused on detecting the illicit shipment of nuclear and radiological materials. Following the events of 9/11, these programs were "augmented by new programs focusing on preventing radiological and nuclear terrorism within the United States. Some of these new and existing efforts had overlapping goals, but they generally used different approaches to improve the detection and security of nuclear materials."[31] For the most part, these programs reside within the Department of Defense (DoD), Energy, and State; agencies that became part of the Department of Homeland Security (DHS) upon its creation in 2002; and the Nuclear Regulatory Commission. Many of these agencies "have both national and international roles in nuclear defense, protecting domestic nuclear assets while aiding in securing or detecting the transport of foreign nuclear material."[32]

While some programs focus primarily on the security of nuclear and radiological materials, other programs have focused on detection of such material in transit in order to ascertain attempts to illicitly transport a nuclear weapon or fissile material across U.S. borders. For example, the DOE Second Line of Defense (SLD) program "aids in establishing capabilities to detect nuclear and radiological materials in foreign countries at ports of entry, border crossings, and other designated locations."[33] Another example is the Department of State Export Control and Related Border Security Assistance Program, which undertakes similar efforts to provide radiation detection capabilities at border crossings.[34]

In addition, there are a variety of programs designed to counter the potential infiltration of nuclear materials in transit toward the United States through screening either at foreign ports or at U.S. borders. The 2007 Homeland Security Strategy identifies four such programs: (1) The Container Security Initiative; (2) The Customs-Trade Partnership Against Terrorism; (3) The Megaports Initiative; and (4) The Secure Freights Initiative.

1. The Container Security Initiative creates a security regime to prescreen and evaluate maritime containers—before they are shipped from foreign ports—through automated targeting tools, ensuring that high-risk cargo is examined or scanned.

2. The Customs-Trade Partnership Against Terrorism is a voluntary U.S. Customs and Border Protection program whereby participating businesses undergo a review of security procedures and adopt enhanced security measures in order to expedite shipping.

3. The Megaports Initiative is a Department of Energy program in which the United States collaborates with foreign trade partners to enhance their ability to scan cargo for nuclear and other radiological materials at major international seaports.

4. The Secure Freight Initiative is a comprehensive model for securing the global supply chain that seeks to enhance security while keeping legitimate trade flowing. It leverages shipper information, host country government partnerships, and trade partnerships to scan cargo containers bound for the United States.[35]

While much attention has been paid to technologies to detect nuclear or radiological material that has been developed or procured by DNDO, port and border security efforts encompass much more than just these sensors. Other elements include the "use of sensor data to inform decision-makers, effective reaction to a detection event, and interdiction of the detected nuclear or radiological material."[36]

Evaluation. According to the U.S. Government Accountability Office (GAO), "combating nuclear smuggling requires an integrated approach that includes equipment, proper training of border security personnel in the use of radiation detection equipment, and intelligence gathering on potential nuclear smuggling operations."[37] Other experts have concluded that "the deployment of radiation detectors needs to be highly integrated with other federal efforts, prioritized on identified threats, configured for flexibility and efficiency, and part of a global approach including international institutions."[38]

In an effort to achieve this objective, the DNDO has attempted to "align existing federal programs so that their capabilities can be compared and integrated into an organizing framework that can help identify gaps and duplication."[39] This coordination by the DNDO allows for a strategy that has the ability to evolve as importation threats that face the United States change in the future. While there has undoubtedly been improvement in port, maritime, and border security, there is still debate among scholars and in Congress over the extent to which newly enacted programs adequately address the severity of the threat.

Detection.

Strategy. In the aftermath of the 9/11 attacks, the U.S. Government sought to prevent the smuggling of nuclear weapons and materials largely through radiation detection. These sensors are designed to reveal radioactive material, and distinguish potentially dangerous fissile material from radiation produced by harmless, everyday substances such as bananas, cat litter, glass, and concrete.[40] The DHS began installing first-generation detector systems in 2002. Since then, more than 800 of the machines have been placed at manned ports of entry, land border crossings, airports, seaports, and international mail facilities.[41] These instruments do not measure the total energy of a container, so while they can gauge the intensity of detected radiation, they cannot measure the characteristic radiation spectrum, or "signature," of a source.[42] Detection is further complicated because highly enriched uranium (HEU)—which, in addition to plutonium, is one of the two materials these sensors are designed to detect—emits a low level of radioactivity that can be easily shielded. For example, when testing current U.S. detection capabilities, the GAO found that encasing a cargo container with radioactive materials in a large amount of scrap metal impeded detection devices installed by the DOE at foreign seaports.[43]

This low level of radioactivity is also problematic because it frequently triggers false alarms when naturally occurring background radiation is confused with HEU. Currently, the United States is developing radiation sensors for use at sensitive locations, but these sensors are also subject to a high rate of false positives. Because of these deficiencies, DHS announced in 2006 that it would acquire hundreds of second-generation radiation detectors designed to reduce false alarms by using technology that would identify a source as harmless radioactive cargo.[44] The following year (FY2007) the Bush administration budgeted $2.8 billion for nuclear detection.[45]

Evaluation. Despite achieving the primary goals of placing radiation detectors at ports in the United States and abroad, the government lacks a plan to plug gaps in nuclear detection to facilitate an effective, holistic strategy.[46] For example, the GAO published a July 2008 report noting that although the DNDO "has taken steps to develop a global nuclear detection architecture," it nonetheless "lacks an overarching strategic plan to help guide how it will achieve a more comprehensive architecture."[47] The report highlights three primary challenges to the successful detection of nuclear materials:

1. U.S.-funded radiological detection programs overseas have proven problematic to implement and sustain and have not been effectively coordinated, although there have been some improvements in this area;

2. Detection technology has limitations and cannot detect and identify all radiological and nuclear materials; and

3. DNDO faces challenges implementing the myriad components of detection. Charged with developing a strategy that depends on programs implemented by other agencies, this responsibility poses a challenge for DNDO in ensuring that the individual programs within the global architecture are effectively integrated and coordinated to maximize the detection and interdiction of radiological or nuclear material.[48]

PART III: RESPONDING TO A NUCLEAR ATTACK

Responding to a nuclear attack in the United States involves three primary components: (1) forensics; (2) immediate response; and (3) consequence management in the days and weeks following an attack. To address each of these elements, this report will first identify the current strategy and then evaluate the strengths and weaknesses of how this planned strategy would be implemented. When analyzing these strategies, one can only speculate so far as their effectiveness is concerned because fortunately the United States has not yet been the victim of a nuclear attack.

Forensics.

Strategy. Tracking down the source of nuclear material after a blast could take several weeks even under ideal conditions, but conducting forensic analysis on a nuclear blast is scientifically possible. During the explosion, the weapon's fissile core would be vaporized and outwardly dispersed with the force of up to 20,000 tons of TNT, depending on the size of the bomb. This cataclysmic event would leave behind traces from which the original bomb's characteristics might be reconstructed.[49]

Developing the capability to determine the source of nuclear material in the aftermath of an attack is currently being spearheaded by the National Technical Nuclear Forensics program (NTNF), which is a joint Homeland Security Council and National Security Council-sponsored policy initiative. The NTNF is designed to establish federal agency missions and institutionalize roles and responsibilities to enable operational support for materials and pre-detonation and post-detonation nuclear or radiological forensics programs.[50]

In addition, the office of NTNF manages the NNSA's technical nuclear forensics assets and capabilities that support nuclear forensics. This office provides the overall program management and the organizational structure in support of technical nuclear forensics for the personnel, equipment, and activities that make up the program. It is responsible for developing and maintaining nuclear forensics operational capabilities for improvised nuclear devices and radiological dispersal devices in support of the Federal Bureau of Investigation (FBI).[51]

Evaluation. Even as the scientific capabilities of the NTNF improve and forensic analysis becomes more advanced, experts agree that the ability to conclusively determine the source of the blast will inevitably be hindered by the lack of an existing national or international catalog of radioactive materials.[52] Charles Ferguson, a scholar at the Council on Foreign Relations, believes that having such a database, even if it contains some gaps, would help ensure that substate actors no longer have "plausible deniability" in the distribution of nuclear materials, which could be an important step towards deterrence.[53]

The lack of information sharing among nuclear states is another factor that hinders successful forensic analysis. While a certain amount of secrecy is undoubtedly necessary to protect a state's nuclear weapon program, "excessive secrecy also precludes states from sharing crucial information about the chemical and isotopic composition of fissile materials stockpiles, which makes attribution in the case of theft or a detonation more difficult."[54]

Whether the United States has the capability to conclusively determine the source of fissile material will substantially impact the range of potential policy responses. Should the United States find, for example, that a state actor supplied the radiological materials necessary to create a nuclear weapon, retaliation against that state sponsor could be considered as a policy option. However, because state actors are sensitive to a calculus of mutually assured destruction, the most likely scenario under which the United States is the target of a nuclear blast is that of an attack by a nonstate actor.[55] This likelihood makes it even more important for the NTNF to be capable of accurately determining the origins of fissile material so that the appropriate balance of statesmanship and security measures can be enacted.

Another reason that it is important to continue to develop the ability to trace any bomb by analyzing its residues is the role of forensics in retaliation. Would the United States strike back against a particular government in the case of nuclear terrorism? Though the temptation to do so might be high, the likelihood of the use of force as a response depends on two variables. First, the United States must have the forensic capability to determine the origin of fissile materials. Second, even if the United States were to positively identify the source of the plutonium or HEU deployed in a blast, "that state might not even be aware that its bombs were stolen or sold, let alone have deliberately provided them to terrorists."[56] For example, retaliating against a major nuclear power, such as Russia or Pakistan, could prove to be counterproductive. Cooperation with one of these governments to put an end to the campaign of nuclear terrorism would be needed to determine who is responsible for the attack.

Immediate Response: The First 24 Hours Following a Nuclear Attack.

The National Strategy for Homeland Security distinguishes between plans of action for *immediate response* and plans of action for *consequence management*. While response refers to "actions taken in the immediate aftermath of an incident to save lives, meet basic human needs, and reduce the loss of property," consequence management is a "broader concept that refers to how we manage incidents and mitigate consequences across all homeland security activities, including prevention, protection, and response and recovery."[57] Similarly, this report will also distinguish between immediate response and consequence management.

Strategy. The National Response Framework[58] (NRF), which became effective in March 2008, details how the United States plans to respond to a variety of emergencies, ranging from a small incident to the largest possible catastrophe, a nuclear attack. This document, which establishes a comprehensive national approach to domestic incident response, identifies the roles and structures that organize national response. It describes how communities, states, the Federal Government, the private sector, and nongovernmental partners apply these principles for an effective coordinated national response. In addition, it describes special circumstances where the Federal Government exercises a larger role, including incidents where federal interests are involved and catastrophic incidents where a state would require significant support—as in the case of a nuclear attack. It lays the groundwork for first responders, decisionmakers, and supporting entities to provide a unified national response.[59]

The NRF states that "an effective, unified national response requires layered, mutually supporting capabilities."[60] The document systematically incorporates public-sector agencies, the private sector, NGOs, and personal preparedness by individuals. There is no doubt that a nuclear attack has the potential to overwhelm even the most prepared local responders from the community, which is why the NRF designates state, federal, and private-sector support teams to coordinate with a community during extreme circumstances.

The specific roles of key partners at the local, state, federal, and private levels are detailed in the NRF, with the main responsibilities as follows:
- Local government and services: The responsibility for responding to a nuclear attack begins at the local level. If possible, these community organizations will provide initial firefighting, law enforcement, emergency medical services, and public works.
- The private sector: Many private-sector organizations are responsible for operating and maintaining portions of the nation's critical infrastructure, such as businesses that provide water, power, communication networks, transportation, medical care, and security.

- NGOs: Many NGOs provide shelter, emergency food supplies, counseling services, and other vital support services to response and promote the recovery of disaster victims.
- State government: The state emergency management agency may dispatch personnel to the scene to assist in the response and recovery effort.
- Federal Government: Because a nuclear attack would exceed local or state resources, the Federal Government will involve all necessary department and agency capabilities and ensure coordination with response partners. The Federal Government's response structures, as outlined in the NRF, will be scalable so that they may adapt to the nature and scope of the attack.[61]

Evaluation. Although nothing in the NRF alters or impedes the ability of federal, state, or local departments to perform their responsibilities, the National Strategy for Homeland Security admits that the United States currently lacks an articulated strategy "for specifically designating roles, responsibilities, and lines of authority for all response stakeholders . . . so that each understands how it supports the broader national response."[62] This lack of specific role designation may be intentional, to allow for a scalable response, but may prove to cause confusion and ambiguity about an agency's jurisdiction to respond.[63]

Experts admit that "there is no silver bullet for planning an effective response" to a nuclear attack, but the current strategy for initial response when dealing with a broad spectrum of homeland security threats assumes that the majority of incidents will be handled at the lowest jurisdictional level possible, with the Federal Government anticipating needs and assisting state and local authorities upon request.[64] However, a nuclear attack would devastate local responders, and would certainly warrant the immediate assistance of the Federal Government. If the government does not anticipate this role, the effectiveness of initial response efforts will be severely compromised.

Without a clear plan of who, from the national level, will respond (for example, federal organizations such as the Nuclear Emergency Support Teams, the Federal Radiological Monitoring and Assessment Center, or the Federal Emergency Management Agency) an effective response may not be organized or executed to the optimal degree. Although the DNDO established a senior policy coordinating body, the Interagency Coordination Council, to address higher level policy issues and further coordinate activities between agencies, the extent to which this body is able to implement and develop new policy for the participating agencies is not known.[65]

Consequence Management.

The transition between initial response, consisting of the immediate actions taken just after an attack, to short-term and long-term consequence management will not be a definitive moment. Instead, the strategies are designed to flow as the needs of individuals, communities, and the nation evolve. Consequence management actions will take place concurrently with all other components of response, including forensics and immediate incident management.

Strategy. Recognizing that the priorities and needs of a catastrophic incident evolve over time, the National Strategy for Homeland Security outlines a plan to reallocate people, assets, and resources in order to provide a flexible response. Other components of the strategy include restoring community services and the economy, organizing planning efforts among key players, facilitating long-term assistance for displaced victims, and rebuilding critical infrastructure.[66]

As with any large-scale disaster, the task of rebuilding and revitalizing communities that have been devastated by a nuclear attack has the potential to overwhelm a state government and take several months and sometimes years, depending on the severity and extent of destruction. As stated in the National Strategy for Homeland Security, some cases might require the complete reconstruction of critical infrastructure and key resources, redevelopment of homes and long-term housing solutions, and the restoration of economic growth and vitality.[67]

No matter how thorough the planning, under no circumstance will we be able to anticipate the precise needs of everyone affected following a nuclear attack. It is, however, worth the effort to try because an organized and clear strategy will "save thousands of lives, billions of dollars, prevent unnecessary panic, help maintain trust in the government, and help preserve democratic institutions in a time of emergency."[68]

Evaluation. Successful consequence management efforts will not be possible without: (1) cooperation among federal, local, and private agencies; and (2) the ability to evolve to meet uncertain and changing circumstances. Complete cooperation between the Federal Government, state and local governments, and the private sector is needed to achieve a sustainable measure of preparedness for the threat of nuclear terrorism. The scale of disaster would require that the state and Federal Governments be prepared to devote all possible resources to the crisis.

The National Strategy for Homeland Security emphasizes the need to reassign people, assets, and resources as needs evolve and incident priorities change. This ability to adapt will be critical to ensure an effective transition to long-term rebuilding and revitalization efforts. Lessons learned from previous domestic emergencies demonstrated the importance of scaling a response to evolving circumstances.

In terms of resource integration, there is some dispute and ambiguity in the literature over whether the local, state, or Federal Government should have primary jurisdiction over the response to a nuclear attack. For example, several authors are of the opinion that "if the nation's top emergency planners are to have any conceivable hope of mitigating the severity of its impact . . . the Federal Government should stop pretending that state and local officials will be able to manage the situation by themselves."[69] They continue:

> Unfortunately, the pretense persists in Washington that the role of the Federal Government in such a scenario is to support governors and mayors, who will retain authority and responsibility in the affected area. Although this is a reasonable application of the federal system to small- and medium-sized emergencies, it is not appropriate for large disasters such as a nuclear detonation. As the fiasco after Hurricane Katrina suggests, most cities and states will quickly be overwhelmed by the magnitude of the humanitarian, law and order, and logistical challenges of responding to a nuclear blast.[70]

The Gilmore Commission, meanwhile, notes the strategic importance of cooperation with the state and local governments, since these authorities are likely to be the first respondents to a nuclear attack. The Commission notes that "the Federal Government should provide resources to states through a single source, based on risk."[71]

PART IV: ANALYSIS — ANSWERING THE FOUR PRIMARY QUESTIONS CENTRAL TO THE PROJECT ON NATIONAL SECURITY REFORM

1. *Did the U.S. Government generally act in an ad hoc manner or did it develop effective strategies to integrate its national security resources?* The National Response Framework (NRF) details how the United States plans to respond to a variety of emergencies, ranging from small incidents to the largest possible catastrophes. In this regard, the United States does have a strategy to integrate national security resources and respond to a nuclear attack, because such an event would fall into the category of a large catastrophe. But whether or not the contingency plans for large catastrophes in general will be adequate for a nuclear attack is unknown. Fortunately the government has not yet had to test the NRF in this capacity. However, due to the severity and urgency of this threat, as well as the resulting devastation peculiar to a nuclear attack, it warrants its own equally comprehensive response plan. Such a plan does yet not exist.[72]

There is no panacea in responding to a nuclear attack.[73] Devastation will inevitably ensue, but the actions of public officials can minimize the destruction. The current strategy for initial response when dealing with a broad spectrum of homeland security threats (as opposed to a strategy that focuses specifically on a nuclear attack) assumes that the majority of incidents will be handled at the lowest possible level, with the Federal Government anticipating needs and assisting state and local authorities upon request.[74] However, a nuclear attack has the potential to devastate local responders, and would certainly warrant the assistance of the Federal Government. If the government does not anticipate this role, the effectiveness of all components of response efforts—including forensics, initial response, and consequence management—will be severely compromised.

Furthermore, "a continuing problem is a lack of clear strategic guidance from the federal level about the definition and objectives of preparedness and how states and localities will be evaluated in meeting those objectives."[75] Until a plan is in place to deal specifically with the response and recovery efforts in the aftermath of a nuclear attack—one that calls for more than a few meetings of advisory groups and articulates requirements and develops priorities from the local level up to the national level—continuing "fragmentation and potential misapplication of resources could result."[76]

2. *How well did the agencies/departments work together to implement these ad hoc or integrated strategies?* Attempts have been made to integrate federal agencies that will be called upon in the aftermath of a nuclear attack. For example, the DNDO has established an Interagency Coordination Council, which includes senior officials from the DoD, the Department of State, the Department of Energy, and the FBI, among other agencies. In preparation for defense against a nuclear attack, the Interagency Coordination Council meets to discuss "strategy planning, policy, and other activities across the Federal Government that require coordination to support national nuclear counterterrorism and

counterproliferation programs and initiatives."⁷⁷ Also, DHS contains a counterpart to the Internal Coordination Council called the Advisory Council; members of the Advisory Council provide DHS guidance to DNDO, and coordinate— intra-agency DHS efforts.

The Interagency Coordination Council is critical for the oversight and implementation of the global nuclear counterterrorism architecture, but a report published by the Congressional Research Service in July 2008 states that procedural and organizational issues may pose barriers to its success. For example, if the Director of DNDO is not equal in authority to the officials in other agencies with whom he is coordinating, his effectiveness may be limited because other officials may have more control of budgets, activities, and policies.⁷⁸ Additionally, other agencies may perceive efforts made by DNDO to coordinate roles and responsibilities as a DNDO initiative rather than a consensus coordination document. If so, these agencies may not adopt the coordinated premises and instead continue to operate under individual agency priorities.⁷⁹

Because there is no comprehensive response plan tailored specifically to a nuclear attack, lead agency responsibilities in the event of such a disaster remain undefined and unclear. In an effort to improve the coherence of interagency efforts, "the Bush administration . . . assigned various players to take the lead in coordinating interagency activities."⁸⁰ However, this effort has not achieved its intended goal and instead has resulted in "a confusing tangle of lead agency responsibilities that complicate rather than unify planning and resource allocation and are bound to sow confusion during emergency operations."⁸¹ To the extent that interagency cooperation occurs today, participants claim that it initiated from "existing, informal networks of personal working relationships that developed decades ago" at various federal agencies rather than from formal arrangements.[82]

3. *What Variables Explain the Strengths and Weaknesses of the Response?* The need for developing and implementing a national, interagency, and intergovernmental strategy for preventing and responding to the various components of a nuclear attack has not gone unrecognized. However, the process of implementing interagency reform and improving a strategy to prevent and respond to a nuclear attack has primarily been hindered by the following factors:

- Limitations in detection technology, which prevent the identification of all radiological and nuclear materials that could illicitly enter the United States via air, land, or sea;
- Lack of an existing national or international catalog of radioactive materials, which hinders our ability to determine the source of a nuclear detonation through forensic analysis;
- Widely varying levels of interest and support for interagency cooperation by federal departments and agencies;
- Fragmentation of responsibilities and capabilities within the federal structure;
- Lack of primary agency responsibility and accountability;
- Inadequate strategic guidance from the federal level about the definition and objectives of preparedness and how states and localities will be held accountable in meeting those objectives;[83]
- Inadequate education, training, and equipment for emergency responders at the local, state and federal levels;[84]

- Lack of a well-defined process for two-way information sharing between federal and state officials regarding strategic decisionmaking;[85]
- Absence of a sustained personal effort by the administration to take a central role in urging and overseeing the execution of interagency coordination efforts;[86] and
- The National Strategy for Homeland Security's acknowledgment that the United States currently lacks an articulated strategy "for specifically designating roles, responsibilities, and lines of authority for all response stakeholders . . . so that each understands how it supports the broader national response."[87]

Each of these factors contributes to the disparity between strategic rhetoric and strategic action. While there has undoubtedly been improvement in recent years, there is still debate among scholars and in Congress over the extent to which newly enacted programs adequately address the severity of the threat of nuclear terrorism.

4. *What diplomatic, financial, and other effects and costs would result from these successes and failures?* Thus far, strategies to prevent a nuclear attack—such as the Cooperative Threat Reduction programs in Russia and the former Soviet Union—have largely proven successful by accomplishing the tasks they were designed to perform. In addition, there has undoubtedly been improvement in port, maritime, and border security.

However, just because a strategy has thus far proven successful does not mean it is flawless. Through the hard work of dedicated individuals, the United States has been successful in preventing a nuclear disaster, but debate continues among national security experts and in Congress over the extent to which newly enacted programs adequately address the severity of the threat.

The fact that the United States has until now avoided a nuclear attack should not result in complacency. It would be a mistake to rely solely on our prevention capabilities and not have a plan in place to respond to a nuclear attack if prevention failed; a single, overarching strategy to respond specifically to a nuclear attack does not yet exist. "This process cannot be effective without a coordinated system for the development, delivery, and administration of various program tasks that engages a broad range of stakeholders."[88] Although no contingency plan, however well conceived or executed, would stop this day from being the most catastrophic single event in the nation's history, "it will nevertheless save thousands of lives, billions of dollars, prevent unnecessary panic, help maintain trust in the government, and help preserve democratic institutions in a time of emergency."[89]

CONCLUSION

The first step in solving any problem is recognizing that a problem exists. As stated in the 2006 National Security Strategy of the United States, the proliferation of nuclear weapons that could result in a nuclear attack on the homeland poses the greatest threat to our national security.[90] This recognition has prompted a vast array of reforms and the establishment of new programs and procedures for both preventing a nuclear attack and responding to catastrophic emergencies. Debate remains among national security experts and in Congress over the extent to which newly enacted programs adequately address the severity and urgency of the threat.

Through the National Response Framework, the United States has outlined a plan for responding to a variety of homeland emergencies, but a strategy detailing how federal agencies would respond to a nuclear attack does not yet exist. Given the unprecedented level of devastation that a nuclear explosion would cause, it is not sufficient to have this threat fall under the umbrella simply of catastrophic emergency management. This lack of specific role designation following such an attack may be intentional to allow for a scalable response, but it may also cause confusion and ambiguity in terms of federal agency jurisdiction and the distinction between the roles of the local, state, and national governments.[91]

Despite bipartisan consensus that nuclear weapons in the hands of terrorists constitute one of the most important threats the nation faces, the United States still lacks an organized, systematic program to improve the quality of national coordination and oversight of its many disparate efforts to meet the threat of nuclear terrorism. Because federal efforts to protect against a nuclear attack are spread among multiple agencies, "determining the full range of existing efforts, coordinating the outcomes of these efforts, identifying any overlaps and gaps between them, and developing an architecture integrating current and future efforts are likely to be evolving, ongoing tasks."[92] A compelling need remains for high-level policy coordination that rises above the inevitable bureaucratic challenges among federal agencies.[93] Furthermore, the need remains for federal cross department coordination, the commitment of sustained executive leadership, and continuing dialogue with local and state elected leaders.[94]

ENDNOTES - CHAPTER 6

1. *The National Security Strategy of the United States*, Washington, DC: The White House, 2006.

2. Dana A. Shea, *The Global Nuclear Detection Architecture: Issues for Congress*, Washington, DC: Congressional Research Service, July 16, 2008, p. 4.

3. Gordon Adams and Cindy Williams, "Strengthening Statecraft and Security: Reforming U.S. Planning and Resource Allocation," Security Studies Program, Cambridge: Massachusetts Institute of Technology, June 2008, p. 27.

4. *Ibid.*

5. The Gilmore Commission Report, "Forging America's New Normalcy," Washington, DC: RAND Corporation, December 15, 2003, p. 5.

6. Homeland Security Council, "Planning Scenarios: Executive Summaries," Washington, DC: HSC, 2004.

7. Gilmore Commission Report, p. 5.

8. Adams and Williams, p. 49.

9. Ashton B. Carter, Michael M. May, and William J. Perry, "The Day After: Action Following a Nuclear Blast In a U.S. City," *The Washington Quarterly*, Autumn 2007, pp. 28-29.

10. United States Senate, "Nuclear Detection: Preliminary Observations on the Domestic Nuclear Detection Office's Efforts to Develop a Global Nuclear Detection Architecture," Committee on Homeland Security and Governmental Affairs, Washington, DC: U.S. Government Accountability Office, 2008, p. 3.

11. *Ibid.*

12. *Ibid.*

13. Federation of American Scientists, "Fact Sheet," April 15, 2005, July, 15 2008, available from *www.fas.org/irp/offdocs/nspd/nspd-43fs.html*.

14. U.S. Department of Energy, "National Nuclear Security Administration: Emergency Operations," August 7, 2008, July 1, 2008, available from *www.doe.gov/nationalsecurity/emergencyresponse.htm*.

15. Graham Allison, *Nuclear Terrorism: The Ultimate Preventable Disaster*, New York: Times Books, Henry Holt and Company, LLC, 2004, p. 178.

16. Carter, May, and Perry.

17. Allison, *Nuclear Terrorism*, p. 68.

18. Office of the President of the United States, "The National Security Strategy of the United States of America," Washington, DC: The White House, March 2006, p. 20.

19. Allison, *Nuclear Terrorism*, p. 68.

20. Henry Sokolski and Thomas Riisager, *Beyond Nunn-Lugar: Curbing the Next Wave of Weapons Proliferation Threats from Russia*, Washington, DC: Nonproliferation Policy Education Center, April 2002.

21. Michael Levi, "Preventing Nuclear and Radiological Terrorism," Washington, DC: The Brookings Institution, 2003, p. 4, available from *www.brookings.edu/papers/2003/1024nuclearweapons_levi.aspx?rssid=north percent20korea*.

22. *The National Security Strategy of the United States of America*, 2006, p. 20.

23. *Ibid.*, p. 21.

24. Sokolski and Riisager, *Beyond Nunn-Lugar*, p. 12.

25. Richard Lugar, "Lugar: Trust Still Needs Verification," *Washington Times*, July 18, 2008.

26. Adams and Williams, p. 49.

27. *Ibid.*, p. 51.

28. *The National Security Strategy of the United States of America*, p. 21.

29. Michael A. Levi, "Deterring Nuclear Terrorism," *Issues in Science and Technology*, Vol. 30, No. 3, Spring 2003, p. 77.

30. *Ibid.*, p. 4.

31. Shea, *Global Nuclear Detection Architecture*, p. 1.

32. *Ibid.*

33. *Ibid.*, p. 2.

34. *Ibid.*

35. Office of the President of the United States, *National Strategy for Homeland Security*, Washington, DC: The White House, October 2007, p. 18.

36. Shea, *Global Nuclear Detection Architecture*, p. 5.

37. *Combating Nuclear Smuggling: Efforts to Deploy Radiation Detection Equipment in the United States and in Other Countries*, GAO-05-840T, Washington, DC: U.S. Government Accountability Office, June 21, 2005.

38. Shea, *Global Nuclear Detection Architecture*, p. 5.

39. *Ibid.*

40. Thomas Cochran and Matthew McKinzie, "Detecting Nuclear Smuggling," *Scientific American*, 2008.

41. *Ibid.*

42. *Ibid.*

43. Committee on Homeland Security, *Nuclear Detection: Preliminary Observations*, p. 5.

44. Cochran and McKinzie.

45. Spencer Hsu, "Costly Weapons Detection Programs Are in Disarray," *Washington Post*, July 16, 2008.

46. *Ibid.*

47. Committee on Homeland Security, "Nuclear Detection: Preliminary Observations," p. 4.

48. *Ibid.*, p. 2.

49. Levi, "Deterring Nuclear Terrorism," p. 77.

50. *National Nuclear Security Administration: Nuclear Forensics*, Washington, DC: U.S. Department of Energy, August 19, 2008, available from *nnsa.energy.gov/emergency_ops/nuclear_forensics.htm*.

51. *Ibid.*

52. Chad Brown, *Transcendental Terrorism and Dirty Bombs: Radiological Weapons Threat Revisited,* Montgomery, AL: Center for Strategy and Technology, Air War College, Maxwell Air Force Base, 2006, p. 20.

53. Matthew B. Stannard, "New tools for a new world order: nuclear forensics touted as method to trace bomb materials, deterrent for rogue nations," *San Francisco Chronicle,* October 29, 2006, available from *www.sfgate.com/cgi-bin/article.cgi?f=/c/a/2006/10/29/MNG32M27K61.DTL*.

54. Brown, *Transcendental Terrorism and Dirty Bombs*, p. 20.

55. Levi, "Deterring Nuclear Terrorism," p. 77.

56. William Perry, Ashton Carter, and Michael May, "After the Bomb," *New York Times*, June 12, 2007.

57. *The National Strategy for Homeland Security*, p. 31.

58. Formerly known as the National Response Plan.

59. "National Response Framework," Washington, DC: U.S. Department of Homeland Security, FEMA, January 2008, p. 1, available from *www.fema.gov/pdf/emergency/nrf/nrf-core.pdf*.

60. *Ibid.*, p. 4.

61. *Ibid.*, pp. 17-25.

62. *The National Strategy for Homeland Security*, p. 32.

63. Gilmore Commission Report, p. 7.

64. Carter, May, and Perry, "The Day After: Action Following a Nuclear Blast."

65. Shea, *Global Nuclear Detection Architecture,* p. 14.

66. "The National Strategy for Homeland Security," p. 38.

67. *Ibid.*, p. 37.

68. Carter, May, and Perry, "The Day After: Action Following a Nuclear Blast."

69. *Ibid.*

70. *Ibid.*

71. Gilmore Commission Report, p. 7.

72. Carter, May, and Perry, "The Day After: Action Following a Nuclear Blast."

73. *Ibid.*

74. Gilmore Commission Report, p. 7.

75. *Ibid.*, p. 5.

76. *Ibid.*, p. 7.

77. "DHS's Domestic Nuclear Detection Office Progress in Integrating Detection Capabilities and Response Protocols," Washington, DC: Department of Homeland Security, Office of the Inspector General, July 16, 2007, available from *www.dhs.gov/xoig/assets/mgmtrpts/OIG_08-19_Dec07.pdf*.

78. Shea, *Global Nuclear Detection Architecture*, p. 14.

79. *Ibid.*

80. Adams and Williams, p. 27.

81. *Ibid.*

82. *Ibid.*

83. Gilmore Commission Report, p. 5.

84. Homeland Security Council, "Planning Scenarios."

85. Gilmore Commission Report, p. 5.

86. Adams and Williams, p. 49.

87. *The National Strategy for Homeland Security*, p. 32.

88. Gilmore Commission Report, p. 7.

89. Carter, May, and Perry, "The Day After: Action Following a Nuclear Blast."

90. *The National Security Strategy of the United States*, 2006 p. 19.

91. Gilmore Commission Report, p. 7.

92. Shea, *Global Nuclear Detection Architecture,* p. 4.

93. Gilmore Commission Report, p. 24.

94. *Ibid.*

APPENDIX A

STRESS TESTING RESULTS

Jim Burke
Carrie Madison
Caylan Ford

Five broad sets of recommendations were proposed by PNSR, herein referred to as (1) Core Reforms; (2) White House Command; (3) Integrated Regional Centers; (4) Decentralized Teams; and (5) Structural Consolidation. To demonstrate the efficacy of these reforms, they were stress tested against each of the Vision Working Group's nine scenarios. The matrix (Figure A-1) illustrates the extent to which each set of proposed reforms to the National Security process contributed to better anticipation, reactions, recovery, and system functions.

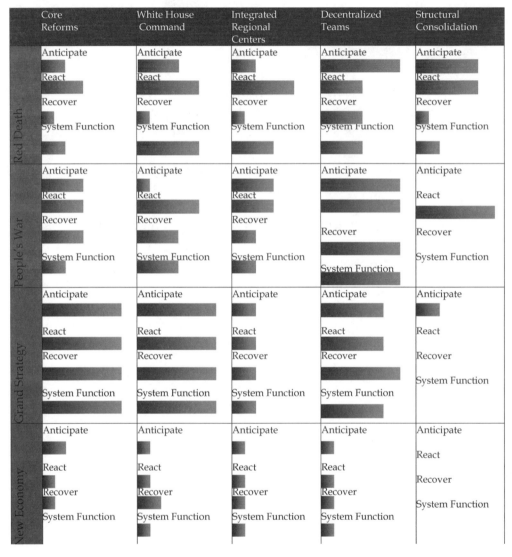

Figure A-1. Matrix Showing Efficacy of Proposed Reforms.

Pax Robotica	Anticipate React Recover System Function	Anticipate React Recover System Function	Anticipate React Recover System Function	Anticipate React Recover System Function	Anticipate React Recover System Function
High Ground	Anticipate React Recover System Function	Anticipate React Recover System Function *	Anticipate React Recover System Function	Anticipate React Recover System Function	Anticipate React Recover System Function
Brave New World	Anticipate React Recover System Function	Anticipate React Recover System Function	Anticipate React Recover System Function	Anticipate React Recover System Function	Anticipate React Recover System Function
Warm Reception	Anticipate React Recover System Function	Anticipate React Recover System Function	Anticipate React Recover System Function	Anticipate React Recover System Function	Anticipate React Recover System Function
Small World	Anticipate React Recover System Function	Anticipate React Recover System Function	Anticipate React Recover System Function	Anticipate React Recover System Function	Anticipate React Recover System Function

Figure A-1. Matrix Showing Efficacy of Proposed Reforms (cont.).

CORE REFORMS

Department and agency autonomy must be complemented with the capacity for whole-of-government solutions.

Strategic Direction and Processes: A series of guidance documents to provide strategic direction; a more powerful National Security Council (NSC) executive secretariat to manage an interagency human capital plan; a National Assessment and Visioning Center and an Office of Decision Support and System; improved budgeting processes to complement enhanced strategic direction.

Human Capital: A National Security Professional Corps to complement department personnel with professionals able to move easily among agencies and into positions requiring interagency experience.

Knowledge Management: 20A Chief Knowledge Officer, heading an Office of Decision Support, to manage common information technology, terminology, and classification systems.

Congress: Senate and House committees for interagency matters; consolidated oversight of the Department of Homeland Security and the intelligence community; strengthened oversight capabilities of supporting organizations (e.g., the Government Accountability Office and the appropriations committees); requirement for Senate confirmation of an executive secretary of the NSC.

These core reforms give the president and his advisors the tools to direct and manage the national security system, while establishing a culture that supports interagency collaboration. However, decentralizing issue management is still necessary to alleviate the president's span-of-control problem. It can be resolved with any of three options as described in the next three broad sets of recommendations.

White House Command: Option One for Alleviating President's Span-of-Control Problem.

Replace the NSC and HSC with the President's Security Council. Create a director for national security (DNS) with super-Cabinet authority on interagency issues with his/her staff running the hierarchy of Washington-based interagency committees.

This approach is familiar, using the ultimate authority of the president to integrate and coordinate, and optimal for an environment dominated by the rivalries between great powers. However, it relies on a talented DNS and staff, would work best with a president skilled in foreign policy and bureaucratic politics, and still leaves the president and DNS with a possibly unmanageable span of control.

Integrated Regional Centers: Option Two.

Shift the existing system's emphasis to the regional level with regional directors heading integrated regional centers (IRCs), which act as interagency headquarters for national security policy. The President's Security Council replaces the NSC and HSC, convening Cabinet members and integrated regional directors based on issues, not statutory membership. The national security advisor and a small staff focus on national strategy and system management, as integrated regional centers manage issues. The departments and agencies support IRCs by providing capabilities.

This option builds on the success of the regional military commands while correcting the current civil-military imbalance by providing a civilian counterpart to the regional commands; it allows Washington to focus on global and long-range policy and strategy; and it gives embassies clear authority to coordinate their country plans. However, global issues would require IRCs to work across their seams on a regular basis. Despite mechanisms to facilitate this, the tendency of IRCs to become independent fiefdoms focused solely on regional issues would be a liability.

A Hierarchy of Decentralized Teams: Option Three.

A hierarchy—national, regional, country—of empowered cross-functional teams manages issues at all levels for the president, conducting issue management on a day-to-day basis.

This option is the most decentralized and collaborative, leaving long-range strategic direction, setting priorities and aligning resources, and moderating issue team efforts as the primary activities of the White House and the president's security advisor and staff. Empowered teams provide for truly integrated courses of action, fix accountability (on the team leader), concentrate expertise, and afford the most flexible response to diverse security challenges. However, teams are management-intensive, and slower to make decisions; their focus on mission accomplishment means they may sacrifice other national objectives to meet their mandates. In addition, teams would work best under the authority of strong structural hubs. Team efforts would have to be carefully delineated, closely monitored, and deconflicted.

Structural Consolidation: Supporting Options.

The three subordinate reforms offered below are primarily, but not exclusively, structural consolidations. All three would be politically challenging but could substantially improve the efficacy of any of the preceding options: 1) an integrated civil-military chain of command in the field when large numbers of U.S. military forces are present; 2) a new Department of International Relations to provide better unity of purpose for soft power; and 3) an empowered Department of Homeland Security to unify effort across the Federal Government in collaboration with state and local authorities.

CONCLUSION

Considered separately or as a whole, these reforms are robust, even radical. They need not be adopted in toto, and hybrid solutions drawing upon some or all of these options are possible. However, the United States will need to adopt some combination of the reforms offered in this paper if it wants a national security system that consistently produces unified purpose and effort.

APPENDIX B

USING SCENARIO-BASED PLANNING TO DEVELOP A VISION OF SUCCESS

Daniel Langberg
Sheila R. Ronis
Robert B. Polk

INTRODUCTION

This appendix examines scenario-based planning and considers the extent to which the U.S. Government or component parts utilize this planning methodology to develop visions of success. Visioning, sometimes called futuring,[1] is considered one of many tools within the overall category of scenario-based planning.

A vision is a detailed description of an organizational system operating "successfully" in some future state. It is not a plan to get there, and it not a simple statement of goals towards that desired state. It is a description in depth of the entire system, all of its parts, working together in that future state successfully. It requires analysis and synthesis across the complex domain of all the moving parts of that system. In the case of a single U.S. department, it would include a complete description of all its internal bureaus, directorates, etc, . . . working together successfully in a future environment. For the whole of the U.S. Government, it would obviously be even more expansive.

"Successfully" is defined by the purpose of the system. For a single department, a successful system would be one that is achieving its highest intended purpose. For the whole of the U.S. Government, it would be a description of all the pertinent departments and agencies working in concert to achieve a particular purpose such as national security. The detailed description would also likely include all the methods and resources necessary for achieving that purpose.

Creating a vision is important because without it a system cannot clearly articulate its ultimate purpose with any granularity nor can it design the processes and outputs necessary to achieve this purpose. The Vision Working Group's description of the current national security system's approach to *scenario-based planning* will contain the following elements: (1) a glossary of key terminology; (2) a short historical overview of scenario-based planning in the U.S. Government; (3) a description of existing U.S. Government visions along with an analysis of the extent to which these were developed using scenario-based methodologies; (4) a summary of current scenario-based planning practices (U.S. Government, United States, and Allied) used for purposes other than developing visions; and (5) a problem analysis focused on assumptions, problems, causes, and consequences.

Scenario-Based Planning. Originally developed by Herman Kahn at the RAND Corporation in Santa Monica, California, scenario-based planning is the use of stories or "conjectures about what might happen in the future."[2]

Scenario. A narrative that describes hypothetical sequences of events constructed for the purpose of focusing attention on causal processes and decision points.[3]

Vision. A form of scenario-based planning that provides a 360 degree description of a system operating successfully in a future state, and the role an individual, institution, government, or state will play in that successful system. A vision:

1. Describes at least one scenario of the future and usually several alternative futures;

2. Describes the role of an organization in the future;

3. Describes a successful role in the future; and

4. Provides a level of granularity from which actionable implications can be derived.

Vision Statement. A concise statement of a vision, usually limited to several sentences.

Mission Statement. A clear, concise statement of an organization's purpose (ends), methods (ways) to achieve that purpose, and resources (means) required.

Forecasting. An analysis of trend data used to predict.[4] "Forecasting is the process of estimation in unknown situations. Prediction is a similar but more general term, and usually refers to estimation of time series, cross sectional, or longitudinal data."[5]

The Current System.

1. Historical Overview.[6] Scenario-based planning has existed in various forms throughout much of history. Following a long-standing tradition in wargaming such as the development of War Plan Orange and the annual GLOBAL series at the U.S. Naval War College, civilian organizations in America first began to utilize this tool through the activities of the RAND Corporation during and after World War II.[7] The term *scenario* (in relation to policy and planning) was coined by Herman Kahn at the RAND Corporation in the 1950s as part of the strategic and military work he was doing for the U.S. Government.[8] The word *scenario* appeared in the civilian public domain in 1967 with

the publication of Kahn's book, *The Year 2000*, with Anthony Wiener. In this book, they defined a scenario as a narrative that described "hypothetical sequences of events constructed for the purpose of focusing attention on causal processes and decision points."[9] Paul Dragos Aligica, a scholar who has written a great deal on scenario use (2004),[10] shows how Kahn's work was prompted by his efforts to find an effective way to undertake interdisciplinary studies which he saw as essential for addressing important future-oriented policy issues. Kahn also believed that there were limitations to taking a purely deductive approach to such issues because of the unknowability of the future. Aligica[11] (2004) indicates that Kahn saw scenarios as unique in their ability to incorporate knowledge from multiple disciplines and to improve the communication between experts. Consequently, Kahn's focus was on building quality scenarios that would lead policymakers and others "to think the unthinkable."

At about the same time, the need for scenarios within an organizational context was also becoming evident. In 1965, Fred Emery and Eric Trist published their seminal article, *The Causal Texture of Organizational Environments,* which argued that the environments of organizations were changing at an increasing rate. Taking a socio-ecological systems perspective, they identified four "ideal" types of environments faced by organizations that graded towards increasing complexity and uncertainty. One of these they called "turbulent," which is a result not only of the interactions of organizations as they compete with each other, but also a consequence of the developments within the environment itself (driven by innovation for example). These turbulent environments were described by Emery and Trist as resembling the "ground in motion."[12]

For managers, the effect was to increase their sense of uncertainty in relation to the future and the external environment. This brought into question the effectiveness of single point forecasts in planning which assumed a relatively stable world.[13] This prompted firms such as GE, SRI International, Royal Dutch Shell, and increasingly others, to seek out alternative long-term planning approaches that could cope with increasing turbulence and the sense of uncertainty it generated.[14] One of the alternate methods they drew on was Kahn's work with scenarios.[15] By 1977, Robert Linneman and Harold Klein found that 15 percent of American Fortune 1000 companies were using scenarios, with this number doubling by 1981.[16] In Europe, a similar survey conducted in 1981 found that 36 percent of the largest companies there were using scenarios.[17] Thus, by the early 1980s, scenarios marked by environmental turbulence were becoming accepted as the norm, that is "the primary format for depicting corporate environmental assessments for planning purposes."[18]

However, it was in 1985, with publication of Michael Porter's book *Competitive Advantage* and two *Harvard Business Review* articles by Pierre Wack, that scenarios grabbed the attention of a wider audience, signaling their adaptation to a commercial and organizational context. It is within the organizational context that most of the development and theorization of scenario practice has since occurred.

2. General Assessment of Performance. The United States has not developed a government-wide method or suite of methods to institutionalize scenario-based planning as a means to develop visions of U.S. Government national security organizations operating successfully as a team in the future. Therefore, it cannot effectively identify strategic capabilities needed to meet future threats and opportunities.

3. Underlying Assumptions:
- Visions are most appropriately developed using scenario-based methodologies.
- Visioning enables the national security system to identify strategic capabilities needed to meet future threats and opportunities.
- Organizations are most effective when they are continuously learning from the visioning process, thus developing a context for decisions and policymaking.

4. Visions in the U.S. Government. It is useful to consider the degree to which visions are developed across the U.S. Government and the extent to which those visions are derived from scenario-based planning methodologies. This analysis will show that the development of visions through the use of long-term scenario-based planning is limited, occuring primarily in the defense and intelligence communities. The majority of visions that are developed across the U.S. Government are not informed by scenario-based planning.

The depth and degree to which departments and agencies attempt to create vision statements vary across the government. On the more progressive end of the spectrum, the Department of Defense (DoD) publishes an overarching department-wide Joint Vision looking out 10 and 20 years as guideposts for the transformation of the Armed Forces and military doctrine. Subordinate departmental components create their own vision statements to nest within the larger context of the joint vision.

On the less progressive end of the spectrum, the Department of Homeland Security (DHS), for example, holds the simple vision, "Preserving our freedoms, protecting America . . we secure our homeland." This vision statement is buttressed by a series of Strategic Goals which are outlined in the Department's Strategic Plan,[19] but the vision of all the parts working together as a whole is never provided.

Another example of a less-than-ideal vision statement is that of the Department of Treasury (DoT):

> To Strive to maintain public trust and confidence in U.S. and international economic and financial systems while building on exemplary leadership, best-in-class processes, and a culture that is characteristic of excellence, integrity, and teamwork to achieve its goals on behalf of the American people.[20]

The DoT goes on to develop common missions, functions, goals, objectives, values, and strategies, but does not elaborate on how these will all come together as a whole in some future state. As a consequence, the organization is left with lists of tasks rather than a complete picture of the operating system. *In some instances, mission statements are used in lieu of vision statements and the terms are used interchangeably.*

The joint Department of State (DoS)/U.S. Agency for International Development (USAID) Strategic Plan for Fiscal Years 2007-12[21] sets forth the following lengthy phrase as its "mission":

> To advance freedom for the benefit of the American people and the international community by helping to build and sustain a more democratic, secure, and prosperous world composed of well-governed states that respond to the needs of their people, reduce widespread poverty, and act responsibly within the international system.[22]

The subsequent DoS/USAID Strategic Plan[23] refers to this "mission" statement as its "vision."

Similarly, the Strategic Plan for the Department of Justice (DoJ) sets forth its mission as follows:

> To enforce the law and defend the interests of the United States according to the law; to ensure public safety against threats foreign and domestic; to provide federal leadership in preventing and controlling crime; to seek just punishment for those guilty of unlawful behavior; and to ensure fair and impartial administration of justice for all Americans.[24]

Later in the document, this mission statement is summarized and referred to as a "vision" for the Department.

In addition to causing confusion, referring to a *mission* and *vision* interchangeably can be a costly mistake. A mission describes in a clear and concise statement an organization's purpose (ends), methods (ways) to achieve that purpose, and the resources (means) required. A vision statement takes that mission statement and puts it into the context of the future and then describes the roles of the organizational parts functioning successfully. The vision statement is less bound by time, potentially remaining the same for decades, while a mission is usually presented as a compilation of more specific and often immediate objectives.

Several other departments such as Justice (DoJ), Health and Human Services (HHS), and Commerce (DoC), have no discernible overarching mission statement or vision but instead are content to let their internal component parts come up with their own. As such, the overarching department becomes a compilation of visions and mission statements rather than a whole in itself.

The following section provides an overview of the extent to which key departments and agencies in the U.S. National Security System have developed vision statements. This summary will focus on DoD, DoS, USAID, DHS, DoJ, DoT, Department of Health and Human Services (DHHS), Department of Agriculture (USDA), DoE, Department of Labor, Department of Commerce (DoC), and Office of the Director of National Intelligence (ODNI).

Department of Defense.

The Department of Defense (DoD) published the *Joint Vision 2020*[25] in May 2000 building on the conceptual framework established in *Joint Vision 2010* to guide transformation of America's Armed Forces. The concepts put forth in the Joint Vision have formed the basis of U.S. military doctrine.

In addition to this Joint Vision, the military services and other component parts of DoD generally publish their own organization-specific vision statements.

The Department of State and the U.S. Agency for International Development.

The Department of State (DoS) and Agency for International Development (USAID) share a Strategic Plan for Fiscal Years 2004 to 2009 which sets forth the Secretary of State's direction and priorities for both organizations in the coming years. The Strategic Plan supports the policy positions set forth by the President in the 2002 National Security Strategy, describing how the Department and USAID will implement U.S. foreign policy and development assistance. The Plan also contains a list of core values shared by DoS and USAID.[26]

Department of Homeland Security.

As indicated earlier the Department of Homeland Security (DHS) sets forth the following vision statement: "Preserving our freedoms, protecting America . . . we secure our homeland." DHS also publishes a Strategic Plan which outlines the following Strategic Goals:
- Awareness—Identify and understand threats, assess vulnerabilities, determine potential impacts, and disseminate timely information to our homeland security partners and the American public.
- Prevention—Detect, deter, and mitigate threats to our homeland.
- Protection—Safeguard our people and their freedoms, critical infrastructure, property, and the economy of our Nation from acts of terrorism, natural disasters, or other emergencies.
- Response—Lead, manage, and coordinate the national response to acts of terrorism, natural disasters, or other emergencies.
- Recovery—Lead national, state, local, and private sector efforts to restore services and rebuild communities after acts of terrorism, natural disasters, or other emergencies.
- Service—Serve the public effectively by facilitating lawful trade, travel, and immigration.
- Organizational Excellence—Value our most important resource, our people. Create a culture that promotes a common identity, innova-

tion, mutual respect, accountability, and teamwork to achieve efficiencies, effectiveness, and operational synergies.[27]

Additionally, the National Preparedness Guidelines published by the DHS contain the National Preparedness Vision, which provides a concise statement of the core preparedness goal for the Nation: "A nation prepared with coordinated capabilities to prevent, protect against, respond to, and recover from all hazards in a way that balances risk with resources and need."[28]

The Guidelines describe this vision statement as "far-reaching," one recognizing that "preparedness requires a coordinated national effort involving every level of government, as well as the private sector, nongovernmental organizations, and individual citizens." The vision also "acknowledges that the Nation cannot achieve total preparedness for every possible contingency and that no two jurisdictions possess identical capability needs."[29] Although this vision statement is published by a single department (DHS), it is somewhat unique in that it represents a *national* vision for preparedness.

Department of Justice.

The Department of Justice (DoJ) does not publish a vision statement. The Department's 2007-2012 Strategic Plan identifies three Strategic Goals:
  1. Prevent Terrorism and Promote the Nation's Security;
  2. Prevent Crime, Enforce Federal Laws, and Represent the Rights and Interests of the American People; and

3. Ensure the Fair and Efficient Administration of Justice.

In addition to the Strategic Goals and a Mission Statement, DoJ publishes a list of core Department values and objectives.[30]

Department of Treasury.

The Treasury Department's published vision statement is to "strive to maintain public trust and confidence in U.S. and international economic and financial systems while building on exemplary leadership, best-in-class processes, and a culture that is characteristic of excellence, integrity, and teamwork to achieve its goals on behalf of the American people."[31]

In addition to identifying Department-wide mission and functions, the Department's Strategic Plan for Fiscal Years 2007-12 identifies Treasury's goals, objectives, core values, and strategies.[32]

Department of Health and Human Services.

The Department of Health and Human Services (DHHS) does not have a single vision or vision statement. As an agency with many components, many individual offices do publish vision statements such as the Center for Disease Control's vision: "Healthy People in a Healthy World — Through Prevention."[33]

DHHS publishes a Strategic Plan with Department-wide goals and objectives. The plan looks out from 2007 to 2012.[34]

Department of Agriculture.

The U.S. Department of Agriculture (USDA) has a vision "to be recognized as a dynamic organization that is able to efficiently provide the integrated program delivery needed to lead a rapidly evolving food and agriculture system."[35]

The Department has created a strategic plan to implement its vision. The framework of this plan depends on these key activities:
- Expanding markets for agricultural products and supporting international economic development;
- Developing alternative markets for agricultural products and activities;
- Providing financing needed to help expand job opportunities and improve housing, utilities, and infrastructure in rural America;
- Enhancing food safety by taking steps to reduce the prevalence of food-borne hazards from farm to table;
- Improving nutrition and health by providing food assistance and nutrition education and promotion; and
- Managing and protecting America's public and private lands working cooperatively with other levels of government and the private sector.

Department of Energy.

The Department of Energy's (DoE) vision statement is to "achieve results in our lifetime ensuring: energy security; nuclear security; science-driven technology revolutions; and one Department of Energy — keeping our commitments."[36]

The Department also maintains five strategic themes and 16 strategic goals which are outlined in a strategic plan.[37]

Department of Labor.

The Department of Labor puts forth the following vision statement:

> We will promote the economic well-being of workers and their families; help them share in the American dream through rising wages, pensions, health benefits, and expanded economic opportunities; and foster safe and healthful workplaces that are free from discrimination.[38]

Four strategic goals provide the framework for the Department of Labor Strategic Plan for the period 2006-2011. These long-term, overarching goals set forth the Department's core functions while reflecting the vision and priorities for the Department.[39]

Department of Commerce.

Although the Department of Commerce does not publish a common vision, or vision statement, several component agencies and offices have individual vision statements such as that of the Bureau of Industry and Security's (BIS) Office of International Programs (OIP): "to work cooperatively in carrying out export control cooperation with other countries to assist them in strengthening and implementing their own export control systems."[40]

Office of the Director of National Intelligence.

The Office of the Director of National Intelligence (ODNI) sets forth this vision: "a unified enterprise of innovative intelligence professionals whose common purpose in defending American lives and interests, and advancing American values, draws strength from our democratic institutions, diversity, and intellectual and technological prowess."[41] ODNI also publishes both a 100-day plan[42] and a 500-day plan[43] for the U.S. Intelligence Community (IC).

The IC lacks the sort of robust interagency process that the U.S. Government needs, but it does have the most sophisticated process developed in the U.S. Government for futures forecasting, though visioning does not occur in the sense that an ideal set of futures are described along with strategies to improve the probabilities that those futures unfold. The following is a further analysis of the IC process as it currently exists:

1. Scenario-Based Planning for Purposes other than Creating a Vision. Scenario-based planning methodologies are employed throughout the U.S. Government, the nation, and among our allies for purposes other than developing a vision of success. These endeavors are useful and illustrate that scenario-based planning has numerous applications. This section provides a brief overview of existing methodologies that could potentially serve as a starting point for developing visions through scenario-based planning.

a. Military Scenario-Based Planning.[44] The U.S. military uses primarily three types of scenario-based planning—those to assist (1) with sizing the force, (2) with training elements of the force, and (3) with addressing potential or ongoing contingencies across all six phases of the operational continuum.

Force Sizing Scenarios. Force sizing scenarios are used within the U.S. military to size the force. Central to these is the Defense Planning Scenario (DPS),[45] developed by OSD and distributed to the military departments and the Joint Staff (JS) through the Defense Planning Guidance (DPG). DPSs depict security threats and corresponding U.S. military missions guided by a strategic-level concept of operation (CONOP). The Secretary of Defense approves a single set of scenarios intended to ensure DoD consistency for studies, war games, and experimentation. The studies are used to inform force sizing decisions that affect authorities and resources in the medium term (5 to 11 years out, commonly referred to as the Future Years Defense Plan or FYDP). Prior to changes made by former Secretary of Defense Donald Rumsfeld, there was an additional set of scenarios for experimentation and planning that operated 15-25 years in the future called the Future Planning Scenario or FPS. Today the DPSs incorporate, based on scenario specific guidance, both time frames.

The Office of the Under Secretary of Defense for Policy (OUSD-P) leads the scenario-building process and has final authority on DPS content. The JS Director for Operational Plans and Interoperability (J7) is responsible for developing the Blue (friendly) Force CONOP and leads a working group with representation from OSD, JS, the Services, and combat support agencies that provide input to the scenario development.

DPSs are used in a variety of force-planning activities including:
- Program and budget analyses
- Major joint studies
- Concept development activities
- Joint, interagency, and combined war games.

DPSs incorporate:
- Problem descriptions, assumptions, and key parameters produced by OSD
- Threat descriptions from the intelligence community
- A CONOP for U.S. forces developed by a JS-led team consisting of Service and other subject-matter experts.

DPSs intend to tie scenarios to future concepts by incorporating the concepts and capabilities outlined in the Joint Operating Concepts (JOCs) and Joint Functional Concepts (JFCs) into the scenarios. The JS/J7 Joint Exercises, Transformation, and Concepts Division (JETCD) oversees the process by which relevant concepts and capabilities are integrated into the Blue CONOP for each scenario. In addition, Joint Integrating Concept (JIC) authors are required to reference a DPS in the development of their document.

Training Scenarios. Training scenarios are used within the U.S. military to train elements of the force. Some are used for joint training, while others are developed by a particular Service or unit. The majority of training scenarios are conducted on an individual basis, outside of an established process for the development of joint training scenarios. These scenarios are designed to support the objectives of the training (e.g., predeployment training, mission rehearsal) or to ensure that the objectives of the exercise are met and may or may not support actual events.

Contingency Planning Scenarios. Contingency Planning Scenarios are used within the U.S. military to address potential or ongoing contingencies across all six phases of the operational continuum. A contingency is "an anticipated situation that likely would involve military forces in response to natural and man-made disasters, terrorists, subversives, military operations by foreign powers, or other situations as directed by the President or [Secretary of Defense]."[46] The Joint Planning and Execution Community (JPEC) uses contingency planning[47] to develop plans for a wide range of situations based on tasks identified in the Contingency Planning Guidance (CPG), Joint Strategic Capabilities Plan (JSCP), and other planning directives. Contingency planning begins when a planning requirement is identified in the CPG, JSCP, or a planning order, and continues until the requirement is met. Based on guidance from the CPG, the JSCP mandates a certain number of contingency plans to be produced and maintained. Specifically, the JSCP:

- Links the Joint Strategic Planning System to joint operation planning;
- Identifies broad scenarios for plan development;
- Specifies the type of joint Operation Plan (OPLAN) required; and
- Provides additional planning guidance as necessary.

A Commander may also initiate contingency planning by preparing plans not specifically assigned but considered necessary to discharge command responsibilities.

b. Homeland Security Scenario-Based Planning. The Homeland Security Council (HSC) — in partnership with the DHS, the federal interagency, and state and local homeland security agencies — has developed 15 all-hazards planning scenarios for use in national, federal, state, and local homeland security preparedness activities. Contained in the National Preparedness Guidelines, the 15 National Planning Scenarios collectively depict the broad range of natural and man-made threats facing our nation and guide overall homeland security planning efforts at all levels of government and with the private sector. They form the basis for national planning, training, investments, and exercises needed to prepare for emergencies of all types.[48]

These scenarios are designed to be the foundational structure for the development of national preparedness standards from which homeland security capabilities can be measured. While these scenarios reflect a rigorous analytical effort by federal, state, and local homeland security experts, it is recognized that refinement and revision over time may be necessary to ensure that the scenarios remain accurate, represent the evolving all-hazards threat picture, and embody the capabilities necessary to respond to domestic incidents.[49]

c. Intelligence Community Scenario-Based Planning.[50]

The U.S. Intelligence Community's Role in Forecasting.[51] The mission of the U.S. Intelligence Community is to "collect, analyze, and disseminate accurate, timely, and objective intelligence, independent of political considerations, to the President and all who make and implement U.S. National Security policy, fight our wars, protect our nation, and enforce our laws."[52] The IC role in forecasting is two-fold—as a producer and a consumer of that intelligence. Forecasting, a form of estimative intelligence, is one principal type of intelligence analysis (others include basic and term) the IC produces to accomplish its mission.

The Director of National Intelligence and intelligence agency and activity directors, however, per the

Intelligence Reform and Terrorism Prevention Act of 2004 (IRTPA), also are consumers of intelligence. They use IC products, such as the National Intelligence Estimate (NIE), to develop strategy and long-range plans that support coordinating and managing the capabilities and resources of the broader IC enterprise. Forecasting is an input to effective visioning and/or scenario-based processes. This discussion provides an overview of the IC role as both a producer and consumer of intelligence as well as recommendations for improving the IC forecasting process and the integration of forecasting products into the interagency strategy, planning, and programming process. The information was gathered through interviews with senior officials in the intelligence elements of the DoD, DHS, and the Office of the Director of National Intelligence.

The Intelligence Community as Producer: Supporting the Interagency Strategy, Programming, & Planning Processes. The National Intelligence Council (NIC), formed in 1979, is the IC's "center for mid-term and long-term strategic thinking,"[53] producing estimative intelligence by drawing on the best available expertise inside and outside of the U.S. Government. The NIC, under the auspices of the Office of the Director of National Intelligence (ODNI), serves as the bridge between the IC and policy communities, provides a source of deep substantive expertise on intelligence matters, and is the chief driver and facilitator of IC analytic collaboration. Comprising 13 National Intelligence Officers (NIO), each with responsibility for a geographic area of the globe (e.g., East Asia or Russia/Eurasia), or a functional—or geographically transcendent—issue (e.g., science and technology or warning), the NIC has developed over time into an all-source center for strategic thinking. The core missions of the

NIC, as identified on its web site, include producing National Intelligence Estimates (NIE); generating new knowledge and insight on a wide range of national security issues; providing substantive counsel to the Director of National Intelligence (DNI) and other senior policymakers; reaching out to nongovernmental experts in academia and the private sector to broaden the IC's perspective; and articulating substantive intelligence priorities and procedures to guide intelligence collection and analysis. In addition to NIEs, the NIC publishes products designed for specific customers and specific purposes, including Intelligence Community Assessments (ICA), Intelligence Community Briefs (ICB), desktop reports, watch lists, conference reports, and Sense of the Community Memorandums (SOCM).[54]

THE NIC

The National Intelligence Estimate and Process.

The principal product through which the IC develops and communicates its judgments about the likely course of future events and identifies implications for U.S. policy is the National Intelligence Estimate (NIE). According to information published by the ODNI, the NIE, published by the NIC, embodies the IC's "most authoritative written judgments on national security issues designed to help U.S. civilian and military leaders develop policies to protect U.S. national security interests. NIEs usually provide information on the current state of affairs in the domestic and/or foreign arena but as a basis or backdrop for primarily 'estimative' analysis—that is, judgments about the likely course of future events and the implications of U.S. policy."[55]

An NIE normally is requested by senior policymakers or congressional leaders and, at times, is self-initiated by the NIC based on key customers' known priority interests. The NIO responsible for the specific geographic region or functional issue produces a concept paper and terms of reference for the NIE. These foundational documents, designed to define the key estimative questions, establish drafting responsibilities, and set the drafting and publication schedule, are circulated throughout the NIC and the Intelligence Community's analytic elements for comment and coordination. Generally, one or more key subject matter experts (SME) responsible for analysis on the topic will be assigned to produce the initial draft text. The draft then is provided to the NIC and the SME community for comment and critique. The refined draft is further honed and coordinated by representatives from Intelligence agencies/entities with both direct and indirect responsibility for the topic through a number of meetings and working sessions. One key responsibility of these representatives is to assess and assign a level of confidence to each key judgment in the NIE. The quality and veracity of sources is discussed with representatives of the National Clandestine Service (NCS) to ensure the draft does not include sources of information that have been recalled or otherwise seriously questioned.[56]

NIEs are approved by the National Intelligence Board (NIB). The NIB is chaired by the DNI and comprises the Heads of responsible Intelligence Community agencies or entities. Following NIB approval, the NIE is presented and briefed to the President, senior policymakers, and other key customers. If required, a sanitized version is produced for key customers who may not have access to highly compartmented versions. The entire process, from an initial request through the satisfactory presentation of information to the requestor, generally takes at least several months.[57]

Global Trends Analysis.

Global Trends 2010. In the Autumn of 1996, the NIC and the Institute for National Strategic Studies held a series of conferences at National Defense University to identify key global trends and their impact on major regions and countries of the globe. The exercise was designed to help describe and assess major drivers and features of the international political landscape as they were judged likely to appear in 2010. Participants in the conferences were drawn from academic institutions, journalism, business, the U.S. Government, and other professions.[58] This effort became the first in a series of recurring self-initiated products, published by the NIC approximately every 4 to 5 years.

Global Trends 2015. Published in December 2000 and the second in this series of futures documents, Global Trends 2015 was developed to provide a longer-term strategic perspective and flexible framework within which to discuss and debate the future. The major contribution of the NIC, assisted by experts from the IC, was to harness U.S. Government and nongovernmental specialists to identify and prioritize drivers, highlight key uncertainties, and produce an integrated trends analysis within a national security context. The resulting product served to identify issues for more rigorous analysis and quantification.[59]

Mapping the Global Future. In this third global trends document, published in late 2004, the NIC continued to refine and provide to U.S. policymakers its assessment of the evolution of international developments and of the threats and opportunities potentially emergent from that evolution which could warrant policy action. Identifying four major scenarios, *Mapping the Global Future* carried the strategic global perspective out to 2020.[60]

NIC 2025. As of this date, the NIC is working through the fourth iteration of its global trends product line. This product was published during the summer of 2008. Since trend analysis is essential to scenario-based planning and visioning processes, this is a critical element.

OTHER IC-WIDE FORECASTING MECHANISMS

Global Futures Forum.

The Global Futures Forum (GFF) is sponsored by the Central Intelligence Agency. According to its web site, the GFF is a multinational, multidisciplinary intelligence community that works at the unclassified level to identify and make sense of emerging transnational threats.[61] Self-organized and self-managed, the GFF seeks to involve a diverse population of officials and SME to stimulate cross-cultural and interdisciplinary thinking and to challenge prevailing assumptions—all in a nonattribution setting. Core members in intelligence and security organizations are joined by selected experts from academia, nongovernmental organizations, and industry. Topic areas, or communities of interest, are established and maintained by polling members annually. As of this writing, the GFF includes the following communities of interest:[62]
- Emerging and Disruptive Technologies
- Foresight and Warning

- Genocide Prevention
- Global Disease
- Illicit Trafficking
- Practice and Organization of Intelligence
- Proliferation
- Radicalization
- Social Networks
- Terrorism and Counterterrorism Studies.

The GFF reports a membership of more than 900 entities, from nearly 40 countries, with plans to expand into Asia during 2008. Table B-1 lists the countries represented today in the GFF.[63]

Argentina	Estonia	Japan	Singapore
Australia	Finland	Latvia	Slovakia
Austria	France	Lithuania	Spain
Belgium	Germany	Luxemburg	Sweden
Bulgaria	Greece	Netherlands	Switzerland
Canada	Hungary	New Zealand	Trinidad & Tobago
Chile	Ireland	Norway	Turkey
Czech Republic	Israel	Poland	United Kingdom
Denmark	Italy	Romania	United States

Table B-1. Countries Represented in the Global Futures Forum, April 2008.

IC Agencies: Customer-Specific Forecasting.

Outside of NIC taskings, individual agencies within the IC are often tasked by their principal customers for forecasting products. The Defense Intelligence Agency, for example, is responsible for providing intelligence forecasts to defense acquisition planners, defense policymakers, and warfighters.[64] As weapons systems and platforms often have life spans measured in decades (e.g., U.S. Navy aircraft carriers and large frame amphibious ships and U.S. Air Force long-range strategic bombers), Defense Intelligence analysts develop long-range, threat-specific forecasts for use by acquisition planners—designers and engineers working to defeat assessed threats and challenges. Further, the IC is often called on to provide technology-specific forecasts for its own use to ensure that future U.S. collection systems can monitor adversary capabilities and challenges. These forecasting efforts are specifically tasked through requirements channels managed by each agency for its unique customer set.

Department-specific efforts to incorporate IC forecasts and future-based threat scenarios as well as those of their organic intelligence elements into their strategy, planning, and programming processes include the Department of Defense (DoD) *Quadrennial Defense Review* (QDR) and the Department of Homeland Security's (DHS) new *Quadrennial Homeland Security Review* (QHSR), modeled after the QDR. The QDR informs both the National Military Strategy, which broadly derives from the National Security Strategy, and the Defense Planning Guidance, which directs specific planning and programming activities in Defense organizations. The QHSR is expected to have a similar role in informing DHS strategy, planning, and programming efforts. The first QHSR will recommend long-term strategies and priorities for homeland security and comprehensively examine programs, assets, budgets, policies, and authorities required to provide the United States with sound, effective future homeland security capabilities.[65]

The Intelligence Community as Consumer: Supporting the IC Enterprise Strategy, Programming, and Planning Processes.

The IC conducts a quadrennial review process, known as the *Quadrennial Intelligence Community Review* (QICR), much the same way the DoD conducts its better known QDR process. Since its 2001 inauguration, the QICR has matured in its use of forecasts and future scenario-based analytic products. Initially, QICR participants consulted NIC Global Trends products, but on an informal basis. Then, as management of the Intelligence Community was reshaped in response to the IRTPA in 2004, the second QICR, conducted in 2005, resulted in "crosstalk among the agencies, but not integration."[66] As the concept and process of enterprise management continues to mature, a key ODNI objective is to improve the synergy and synchronicity between the NIC forecasting process/products and the ODNI strategy and planning process for prioritizing, programming for, and building intelligence capabilities in the out years. During the remainder of 2008, the IC undertook a significant strategic planning regimen led by the ODNI's Office of Strategy, Plans, and Policy. Relying on the NIC's draft product *Global Trends 2025*, the IC undertook an integrated and synchronized strategy formulation and planning process to be completed before the 2009 transition to a new administration.

As depicted in Figure B-1,[67] the Strategic Enterprise Management (SEM) process will use the NIC 2025 product as a catalyst for the next QICR which, in turn, will serve as the underpinning for an integrated Long-Term Programming and Planning Guidance memorandum to be issued by the Director of National Intelligence to the agency heads and managers responsible for execution of the National Intelligence Program (NIP). The strategic planning process will begin with the development and publication of the second National Intelligence Strategy and development of a Single Integrated Priorities List for the IC. The sequence of events, from forecasting through strategic planning, is designed to lead to better informed portfolio investment decisions and establish outcome goals for the NIP.[68]

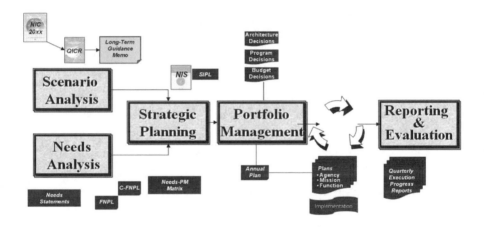

Figure B-1. Intelligence Community Strategic Enterprise Management (SEM) Process.[69]

Challenges.

A recurring theme throughout interviews with senior IC officials is the lack of a single responsible office or official to initiate, synchronize, and lead interagency integration of IC forecasting efforts from the top down. While most, if not all, agreed that Project Horizon is the best approach to date for integrating forecasting into interagency planning,[70] it, too, falls short. Led by the Department of State, the Project Horizon process, which will be discussed separately later in this paper, relies on a cooperative agreement among peers and voluntary participation by the various agencies and organizations of the U.S. Government. Without directive senior leadership and strong buy-in at a level above individual department and agency level, participation and outcomes in such efforts have not translated into authoritative mandates for policy or program changes and/or budget allocations.[71]

Much of what needs to be done in IC forecasting is being done; however, by many estimates, it is being accomplished in a less than optimal environment — one emphasizing analysis of the "threat du jour," meaning short-term preoccupations, or whatever is popular, e.g., Islamic terror or global warming. One senior intelligence official noted that "there are significant 'islands' of futurists and scenario-based planning in the IC, but I would not call it a predominant element of the overall intellectual culture or habit of the community," and "there is still the need to reconcile individual component futures with a community future."[72]

Another challenge is the generally "distant relationship" between most IC analysts and their policymaker customers. As senior analysts attempt to "dialogue" with their customers to better understand their needs and assist them in "contextually articulating" their concerns, some analysts can lose — or can be perceived to have lost — their objectivity, or to be "politicizing" their analysis. This "tension,"[73] created by the competing forces of engaging the customer in the forecasting process while concurrently maintaining an unbiased, objective perspective, or judgments that are "independent of political considerations,"[74] can have a "chilling effect on intelligence managers' support for direct analyst-customer interface. The distance between analysts and customers is often detrimental to the overall process and outcome."[75]

"The customer's requirement for both *accuracy* and *prediction* — often a conflicting requirement when dealing with futures analysis, makes the analyst-customer interface even more significant"[76] when developing a forecast or estimate to ensure that the often nuanced intelligence terminology, types, and range of uncertainty, source reliability, and overall confidence level in the key judgments are well understood. The IC mission, to "collect, analyze, and disseminate accurate, timely, and objective intelligence"[77] requires a mature and effective blend of both art and science. As importantly, customers must understand that intelligence — particularly futures intelligence — *is* as much art as science, and use it with the same care and attention to linguistic detail with which it was developed.[78]

d. U.S. Government-Developed Scenario-Based Planning Methodologies.[79]

Project Horizon.

Recognizing that the wider Federal Government lacked integrated strategic planning mechanisms to reach common goals, the State Department initiated Project Horizon.[80] Specifically, this project was created by the State Department's Office of Strategic and Performance Planning in coordination with the DHS, DoD, and other interagency partners who experimented with the use of scenarios to help with such integration.

According to the Project's Summer 2006 progress report:

Project Horizon has brought together [U.S. Government] senior officials from the National Security Council and Global Affairs agencies to explore ways to improve U.S. Government interagency coordination in global affairs using scenario-based planning. The purpose of the ongoing project is threefold. First, it is to develop strategic interagency capabilities in which the [U.S. Government] should consider investing in order to prepare for the threats and opportunities that will face the nation over the next 20 years. Second, it is to provide participating agencies with a scenario planning toolset that can be used to support both internal agency planning and planning across agencies. Finally, it is to provide a starting point for an institutionalized interagency planning process.[81]

The Project consists of four phases: Phase 1—Scenario Development; Phase 2—Interagency Planning Workshops; Phase 3—Knowledge Transfer; and Phase 4—Agency-specific Planning and Interagency Linkage Analysis.

The project's scenario-based strategic planning methodology is grounded in the assumption that it is impossible to predict long-term futures. Accordingly, "the Project Horizon Core Team systematically created a set of five plausible alternative future operating environments or scenarios based on research and interviews with approximately 200 senior executives from the participating agencies as well as global affairs experts from academia, think tanks, and the private sector."[82] The Project's Progress Report further explains:

> The five Project Horizon scenarios represent a diverse range of operating environments that the U.S. Govern-

ment could face in 2025. They are not intended to be forecasts of the future, and are "valid" only as a set. They are a single planning instrument comprised of five pieces. Each of the scenarios . . . contains distinct challenges and opportunities for the U.S. Government that became the context for the interagency strategic conversations that took place during the Project Horizon planning workshops.[83]

Project Horizon is jointly funded and administered by the following participating organizations: U.S. Department of Agriculture (USDA), Department of Commerce (DoC), Department of Defense (DoD), Department of Energy (DoE), Department of Health and Human Services (DHHS), Department of Homeland Security (DHS), Department of Labor (DoL), Department of State (DoS), Department of Treasury (DoTr), Environmental Protection Agency (EPA), Office of the Director of National Intelligence (ODNI), Millennium Challenge Corporation (MCC), National Defense University NDU), and the U.S. Agency for International Development (USAID).[84]

The Project aims to produce a structured set of interagency strategies, associated considerations, and action plans for:
- Interagency capabilities and tools,
- Organizational models and processes,
- Management and operational models,
- Knowledge, skill, and training requirements, and
- Strategic planning approaches and goal frameworks.

Project Horizon's strategies are designed to address a range of interagency planning issues including global security, development, trade, health, resource management, and humanitarian relief. The Project will also produce a strategic planning toolkit that will enable participating agencies to apply the methodology within their respective organizations and will serve as the foundation for an ongoing interagency strategic planning process. Project Horizon was not intended to produce a holistic "vision" for the U.S. Government.

Although Project Horizon demonstrated a "proof of concept," it has not been institutionalized; nor has it consistently been used with any other visioning or scenario-based tools to provide strategic guidance across the U.S. Government for use in the national security community or any other interagency communities.

UNITED STATES INSTITUTE OF PEACE (USIP) SCENARIO USE

United States Institute of Peace (USIP) has developed simulations[85] which serve primarily as educational tools allowing students to role-play the perspective of key stakeholders in a given scenario. Simulations are designed to increase participants' understanding of peacemaking dynamics. The simulations enable participants to practice the skills of conflict prevention management, and to test policy options to determine the preferred response to a given set of circumstances.

The Strategic Economic Needs and Security Exercise (SENSE),[86] originally developed by the Institute for Defense Analyses (IDA) as the synthetic environment for National Security Estimates (prompted by the need to teach fledgling democratic governments in the Balkans about policy development, market economics, and representative government),[87] and now maintained and employed through USIP, is a computer-based simulation that focuses on negotiations and decisionmaking in a post-conflict environment. SENSE simulates the resource allocation challenges confronting national and international decisionmakers. The simulation provides participants with rapid feedback on the results of their time-sensitive decisionmaking aimed at building political stability, social justice, and a foundation for economic progress. However, the primary activity in SENSE is negotiation between and among those participating in the simulation. SENSE has been used in the Balkans, the Caucasus, Iraq, the United States, and Poland.

An older USIP-developed scenario-based simulation was developed on conflict prevention in the Greater Horn of Africa which focused on preventing the further spread of conflict along the Ethiopia-Eritrea border.[88] The simulation was based on the assumption that the Organization of African Unity (OAU) (which became the African Union as of the Lome Summit of 2000)[89] had established a peace plan to which the two parties in conflict have agreed, and participants were asked, in their roles as representatives of OAU member states, to devise a plan for preventing the spread of the conflict into neighboring countries and the entire region. The issue of refugees and internally displaced persons present a humanitarian crisis that can affect the political and economic stability of the region.

    e. U.S. Non-Government-Developed Scenario-Based Planning Methodologies.[90]

The Strategic Management System (STRATMAS)[91] is a scenario-based simulation designed to provide insight into the effects of key decisions on societal factors. First, a synthetic country is created and a scenario is defined based on real actors and events. Participants design operational plans which are applied to the synthetic country. The model then generates synthetic country responses.

STRATMAS was used to assess the effectiveness of proposed plans for Afghanistan. The study was based on the assumption that the situation in Afghanistan had deteriorated to the point where the NATO-led International Security Assistance Force (ISAF) could no longer be effective. STRATMAS-generated data has provided insight to events in Afghanistan involving the activities of the Afghanistan Emergency Force (AFGEM), the Afghanistan Recovery and Stabilization Force (AFGRES), and other deployed civilian entities in terms of their impact on selected key societal variables. The model is also being used for Iraq. An enhanced version of STRATMAS was used to support JFCOM's Multinational Experiment (MNE) 4. According to one of the model's developers,[92] the system was preferred to the three alternatives due to its ability to identify quick-impact results of data input.

Senturion. The Senturion[93] model provides a capability to map the positions of key stakeholders in a conflict and identifies opportunities to reach an agreement.[94] The model uses input data from subject matter experts (SMEs) to frame issues and to identify stakeholders' positions, influence, and importance. The model applies game theory, decision theory, and spatial bargaining models to simulate:
- Evolving stakeholder relationships,
- The formation of potential coalitions, and
- The impacts of changes in environment.

Senturion can be used to:
- Provide a visual representation of complex situations,

- Integrate the views of the IC,
- Provide insights into complex decisionmaking, and
- Identify 2nd and 3rd order effects of decisions.

The Senturion model has been used in the past for:
- Strategic communications and influence planning,
- Support for deliberate and crisis action planning, and
- Wargaming and exercise support.[95]

Synthetic Environments for Analysis and Simulations.

Developed by Purdue University and marketed by Simulex, Inc., the synthetic environments for analysis and simulations (SEAS)[96] were originally designed for military wargaming exercises and have been expanded to incorporate research from the fields of management, economics, and psychology. According to Simulex, the model provides a user-friendly technology that combines visual interfaces and complex artificial intelligence to produce something that is half simulation and half wargame. SEAS is used by senior officials to game decisions and solve problems ranging from business strategies to disaster management. As an agent-based modeling construct, it re-creates in detail many of the dynamics of a decisionmaking environment while participants re-create the human aspects of interaction. Although SEAS allows for the incorporation of models from multiple domains (social, political, economic, etc.), like SENSE (an IDA-developed model), the model is focused on human interactivity. SEAS was used in Multinational Experiment 4 as a tool to predict in real time the effects of influences on populations to model everything from national reactions to U.S. policy to turbulence within refugee camps.

Conflict Modeling, Planning, and Outcomes Experimentation Program.

The Conflict Modeling, Planning, and Outcomes Experimentation Program (COMPOEX)[97] is a set of models and simulations that acts as a predictive tool to help decisionmakers to see the effects of decisions.[98] The package consists of a conflict space tool (to map sources of instability and relationship and centers of power), a campaign planning tool, an options exploration tool, and a family of models. The complete set aims to identify risk areas and allow users to experiment with risk management strategies by changing variables.

Politics of Fertility and Economic Development Model.

Through the use of pooled data, the Politics of Fertility and Economic Development (POFED) model[99] attempts to identify and estimate the relative impact of a variety of structural variables that contribute to a humanitarian crisis. As a planning tool, POFED provides regional mapping of factors that may contribute to a reduction of instability. The model also helps to identify possible U.S. Government actions that might increase stability and mitigate humanitarian concerns in crisis situations at both the national and subnational levels.

Model output can be simplified for forecasting purposes to anticipate trouble areas, possible consequences of policy changes, and recovery from natural or man-made disaster. Forecasts can be used to describe future scenarios and subsequently identify courses of action to achieve desired policy outcomes.

The majority of POFED indicators are derived from the open source domain. Once a country or situation has been added to the POFED database, automatic annual or quarterly updates are provided easily upon request. Recent applications[100] of POFED include:
- Regional stability in the Horn of Africa,
- Cross-temporal prospects for stability in Sudan,
- Assessment of provincial stability by province in Sudan,
- Evaluation of implications of potential partition in Sudan, and
- Link to stakeholder model (Senturion) to evaluate policy options.

f. Allied Scenario-Based Methodologies.[101]

U.S. Center for Research and Education on Strategy and Technology Working Group on Conflict Prevention.

In early 2006, the U.S. Center for Research and Education on Strategy and Technology (U.S.-CREST) initiated its Coalition Stability Operations (CSO) project focused on multinational stability operations. Sponsored by JFCOM J9, the overarching goal of the project is "to contribute to the definition of more coherent civil-military conceptual approaches and capabilities between European actors and the United States, in an operational domain of increasing importance."[102]

The project's second phase, launched in July 2006, is designed to "bring together several multinational working groups in order to discuss the concepts, capabilities, and coordination mechanisms that are necessary to improve multinational action in stability operations."[103] The first meeting of the project's second phase was held in Paris, France, in December 2006 and focused on the role of the military within a comprehensive approach to conflict prevention. Participants included government officials from France, Italy, the United States, the UK, and representatives from the EU, UN, NATO, OECD, various NGOs, as well as subject matter experts from academia and business. A fictional scenario[104] based in West Africa provided the context for a discussion of the military's contribution to multinational conflict prevention.[105]

EU MILEX 07 Scenario.

The European Union (EU) conducted its second military exercise (MILEX 07)[106] in June 2007. MILEX was a Command Post Exercise (CPX) which focused on the military role in crisis management. During the exercise, the EU Operations Centre (EU OpsCentre), comprised of a military and civilian component, was activated for the first time. No troops were deployed during the exercise.

MILEX 07 was based on a recently developed scenario (ALISIA) that is being used for EU exercises through 2010. The scenario depicts a fictitious country in which tension between the transitional government and a rebel group has led to a humanitarian crisis. A UN mission already on the ground does not have sufficient resources to address the situation and has requested support in the form of an EU operation that will provide the UN with sufficient time to reorganize its personnel. The EU operation includes the deployment of up to 2000 personnel including an Integrated Police Unit (IPU) which has been temporarily placed under military responsibility. The focus of the exercise was on the interaction between the EU OpsCentre in Brussels and the EU Force Headquarters in Sweden.[107]

GMU Conflict Prevention Scenarios Developed for NATO.

The George Mason University (GMU) Peace Operations Policy Program (POPP) developed a series of force planning scenarios[108] for NATO in 2002 in support of the Defense Requirements Review (DRR) for Crisis Response Operations (CRO). The DRR process occurs every 2 years for the purpose of force structuring. A set of scenarios is developed which describe either Article 5 or non-Article 5 (CRO) mission types, which then serve as the basis for a task analysis used to determine force requirements.

Peace Team Forum Scenarios.

The Peace Team Forum[109] is a network of approximately 50 Swedish Human Rights, Humanitarian, and Development organizations. Initiated in August 2005 with funding from the Swedish International Development Agency (SIDA), a coalition of 10 organizations together with the Folke Bernadotte Academy developed a scenario-based exercise on the prevention of armed conflict.[110] The Swedish Armed Forces host a biannual international Peacekeeping exercise and the Swedish Wargaming Center has developed a fictive country called Bogaland for that specific purpose. The

Wargaming center has allowed the Peace Team Forum to use Bogaland and has assisted in the creation of a civil society in the scenario which will be used in future exercises.

The scenario allows participants to develop and test new strategies to address conflict in communities or states at risk of resorting to armed conflict. It serves as a platform for discussion and interaction to confront the challenges of managing dynamic and unpredictable situations in a complex political environment.

PROBLEM ANALYSIS

The preceding sections are intended to demonstrate that: (1) the vast majority of the U.S. Government components and certainly the national security "system" as a whole do not have visions as generally defined; and (2) those components using scenario-based planning, with the sole exception of the DoD, are doing so for reasons other than for interagency planning and execution toward a vision. This discussion outlines the problems, causes, and consequences associated with the lack of an institutionalized government-wide capacity to use scenario-based planning to develop visions of success.

1. *Overview.*

Overall Symptom—National security organizations are rarely prepared, organized, and/or resourced to address emerging national security challenges.

Overarching Problem—The national security system does not have a core competence in strategic visioning. Consequence: The national security system cannot identify strategic capabilities needed to meet future threats and opportunities.

Problem 1 — There are many obstacles to building a core competence in strategic visioning using scenario-based planning.

Cause 1a — There is no overarching process, forum, or venue in which a vision could be developed.

— The national security system has not developed a government-wide method (or suite of methods) to institutionalize scenario-based planning.

Cause 1b — Scenario-based planning can be resource intensive (expensive).

Cause 1c — People do not have time to work on scenario-based planning because of the excessive demands of daily work.

— The vast majority of civilian agencies lack even a single billet devoted to scenario-based planning.

Cause 1d — Scenario-based planning is difficult.

Cause 1e — The departmental focus in the national security system results in an inability to think holistically about planning for the future.

— The national security system has not developed the capacity to plan across the departments and agencies so that strategies can be developed and executed.

Cause 1f — The competition among the departments produces disincentives for government-wide planning.

Cause 1g — It would take years to develop the baseline of national security system capacities and capabilities needed to gain the full benefit of scenario-based planning.

Cause 1h — Planning is not a skill possessed by most elements of the national security system.

— There are no institutional incentives for planning.

Problem 2 — There is a misunderstanding of what a vision is and the value it brings.

Cause 2a—Visioning remains either intimidating or an enigma to many national security professionals, who fail to understand that visioning is not about predicting, but gaining insights into possibilities.

Problem 3—The need for scenario-based planning is not widely understood.

Cause 3a—Many hold a view that future concerns are already well known.

Cause 3b—Many believe that they don't need to build a common view of the future and how they need to fit into the whole.

Cause 3c—Many lack the experience of operating as a team with those in other bureaus or departments.

Problem 4—The national security system rewards short-term results over long-term results.

Cause 4a—The United States has always had a culture of the immediate.

Cause 4b—The national security system has emphasized crisis management and neglected threat management.

Problem 5—Without means for matching resources to strategy, the national security system would be unable to act on scenario-based planning's insights for solution sets.

2. *Isolating Symptoms, Core Problems, and Causes.*

Overall Symptom—National security organizations are rarely prepared, organized, and/or resourced to address emerging national security challenges.

Overarching Problem—The national security system does not have a core competence in strategic visioning.

Problem 1—There are many obstacles to building a core competence in strategic visioning using scenario-based planning.

Cause 1a — There is no overarching process, forum, or venue in which a vision could be developed.

There is currently no established whole-of-government process and forum to enable the development of a common vision for the U.S. National Security System, the U.S. Government, or the nation. In addition to the absence of a government-wide vision, there is currently no overarching process, forum, or venue in which a vision could be developed. The development of such a vision would require a process, forum, and venue that truly transcended individual departmental or agency biases and perspectives. The only such forum that arguably exists today is the National Security Council (NSC) and its system of Policy Coordinating Committees (PCCs). The PCC system could provide a very rudimentary capacity to start a visioning process but to date this system has not been used to mobilize a whole-of-government effort in behalf of visioning or planning. The PCC process is much more geared to the daily inbox or short-term issues and attainment of specific goals for any administration. A much more robust, systemic, and persistent capability is needed in the executive branch.

— The national security system has not developed a government-wide method (or suite of methods) to institutionalize scenario-based planning.

The United States has not developed a government-wide method or suite of methods to institutionalize scenario-based planning as a means to develop visions of U.S. Government national security organizations operating successfully as a team in the future.

Cause 1b — Scenario-based planning can be resource-intensive (expensive). This makes scenario-based planning the exception rather than the rule and accessible only to those who have the necessary funding. Scenario-based planning requires time, information gained through broad and participatory research methods, location for integration, red-teaming, basic expert planning facilitation, and creative writing and thinking. All of these require funding.

Cause 1c — People do not have time to work on scenario-based planning because of the excessive demands of daily work.

— The vast majority of civilian agencies lack even a single billet devoted to scenario-based planning.

The majority of U.S. Government components do not have the overhead in time or people to participate in robust scenario play, being overburdened with their daily work. For both operating and planning outside their quotidian routines, the vast majority of the civilian agencies lack even a single billet to expend on scenario-based planning. Every time the "center" asks of the "edges" for participation in planning or operating outside their own circumscribed mandates, the "edges" or the vast majority of departments and agencies have no funds. Many have called on Congress to rectify this with authorizing and funding a five percent overhead in the domestic departments so that they can participate in such activities as scenario-based planning, extra training, and deployments abroad. All of this, unfortunately, has been to no avail. The result again for scenario-based planning is that it remains a casualty of prioritization.

Cause 1d — Scenario-based planning is difficult.

Scenario-based planning is rigorous intellectual work making it difficult to translate the results of scenario-based planning into a vision. There is not always a one-to-one correlation between cause and effect. Systems are always complex, while unknown environmental factors are an everyday aspect of futuring. In any case, analysis and synthesis are prerequisites. This makes creating a vision less desirable to policymakers and planners who may be looking for immediate results.

Cause 1e—The departmental focus in the national security system results in an inability to think holistically about planning for the future.

—The national security system has not developed the capacity to plan across the departments and agencies so that strategies can be developed and executed.

The stove-piped U.S. Government inhibits the ability to reconcile differences between the way one department sees the future and others see it. There is no doubt that word is out about the myriad of problems associated with a stove piped U.S. Government. Not the least of these, however, is that this reality perpetuates an inability to think holistically about anything, including planning for today and the future. As a result, scenario-based planning becomes the casualty of no planning at all in many agencies and departments.

Cause 1f—The competition among the departments produces disincentives for government-wide planning.

The inability to plan together as a team is rooted in both the nature of departmental competition and survival, and the privileges and powers of the office of the President. In the former, no department wishes to concede any authorities over any issues in a way that might affect funding. Planning together is often seen as giving in by some. In the latter, a struggle between executive lawyers and oversight mechanisms of the legislature is sure to ensue.

Cause 1g—It would take years to develop the baseline of national security system capacities and capabilities needed to gain the full benefit of scenario-based planning.

There is no unified, accessible mapping of U.S. Government capabilities and capacities. Without a better whole-of-government mapping of U.S. Government capacities, policymakers and planners continue to struggle with both understanding the problems and their potential solutions. Can one imagine Toyota or Microsoft looking into the future and considering innovation without knowledge of its own baseline? Neither could government innovators follow up scenario-based planning with recommendations to policymakers without a baseline of their own. This all has a chilling effect on the desire to even try to use scenario-based planning. Mapping the U.S. Government capabilities would requires resources and years of analysis to capture, store, and maintain updated information of this kind. To date, there is no such repository even if the information were collected.

Cause 1h—Planning is not a skill possessed by most elements of the national security system.

Planning of any kind, let alone strategic scenario-based planning is not a skill widely held inside U.S. Government departments. Excepting USAID, DoD, and some parts of DoS, for the U.S. Government's 200-plus departments, agencies, boards, and commissions, planning is at most an afterthought. The result of a lack of planning, scenario-based or otherwise, inside the majority of U.S. Government components is a serious obstacle connected to all the other causes of government incoherency discussed in this document. No one part is enough by itself to make for a successful system. That said, of all the issues, this one may be the most solvable. The skills are potentially there, but the incentives and then the funding to make them emerge and flower across the whole of the U.S. Government are not yet there. The result will likely be a set of piecemeal solution sets offered on scenario-based planning. Some departments will continue to advance in this arena while the majority will fall further behind. In the end, the U.S. Government will struggle with creating any whole-of-government strategies that can lift the entire system up towards a better vision of itself.

—There are no institutional incentives for planning built into the cultures of our government organizations. Such incentives never materialized because most departments were never given a mandate and set of roles and responsibilities that required them to plan and submit their plans to the NSC, as was done with the DoD. This never happened because Congress never understood national security to be much broader than the DoD and perhaps the intelligence agencies. The neglected departments, also as a result, never developed a sense of the need to work with other departments in a whole-of-government plan to accomplish the U.S. missions in Iraq until recently. The only way this will change is if such a capacity to plan is deemed an essential requirement of national security.

Problem 2—There is a misunderstanding of what a vision is and the value it brings.

Many believe that the National Security Strategy (NSS)[111] is a national vision. While the NSS outlines the major national security concerns of the United States and describes generally how the administration plans to deal with them, it is not a vision. Submitted to Congress as a declaration of the administration's policy, it does not describe how all the parts will come together as a whole to successfully achieve an overarching purpose in the future. The word "vision" is mentioned in the Strategy six times, four in the context of a U.S. vision. In none of these instances, however, does the document refer to a single overarching vision for the United States. It uses the term in the context of U.S. "visions" for particular countries such as South Korea, or a broad issue such as on "the global economy." Neither approach comes close to a vision in the true sense of the term.

This belief in the NSS as a national vision is born of a misunderstanding of what a vision is and the value it brings. With understanding of the value added, the adjustments necessary to achieve a true National Security vision can be made.

Most individual departments and agencies confuse vision or mission statements with a true vision and so never consider the necessity of scenario-based planning as an integral part of creating such a vision. Properly constructed, a vision is a description of an organization functioning successfully in a future state. A vision statement (sometimes confused with a mission statement) is a step in the right direction but falls short of the granularity required to derive implications for organizational design and process that a true scenario-based planning process would reveal. A vision is not meant to be left on posters and banners as a rallying cry for positive thinking. It is, rather, a serious document of substance in which all parts can clearly be seen as mechanisms working together in a detailed collaboration of time and resources. Vision Statements and Mission Statements are at best a bumper sticker by comparison. In the absence of a government-wide vision derived from scenario-based planning, department and agency level visions and plans will rarely reinforce and will potentially even contradict one another.

Cause 2a—Visioning remains either intimidating or an enigma to many national security professionals.

Scenario-based planning is considered a new tool to too many government employees, and it thus sounds extremely intimidating to many within the U.S. Government. No doubt others who have had some exposure by participating in DoD-run experiments, exercises, and gaming have come away with mixed feelings of the value of individual experiences. Still others appreciate the demonstrated utility. Often the final results are not even known to the participants, as the hosts usually benefit the most by using the results for internal use. Consequently, socialization of the benefits may be less than it could be. With a combination of mixed results by the few who have participated and zero results by the many more who have never experienced scenario-based planning, it is not surprising that it remains ominously mysterious.

—Not about predicting, but gaining insights into possibilities.

Scenario-based planning has often been confused with predicting the future. There are relatively few examples of how the U.S. Government got it right in preparing for the future ahead of time. Negative examples have dominated the news media and our collective consciousness. Critics revel in government planning gone wrong. Though history has not shown many examples of where we got it right ahead of time, there are such cases. That said, it is the nature of the future for us not to get it perfectly right. But to push this line of thinking too far would be to forever miss the point of scenario-based planning. It is the planning, not the plan, that is important. Even the most strident critics would have to concede to this point, or at least to the point that if we do nothing we risk more than if we at least try to learn from the effort.

Problem 3—The need for scenario-based planning is not widely understood.

Cause 3a—Many hold the view that future concerns are already well known.

Many in government believe that the future concerns that need addressing are already understood. As a result, they may not feel the need to build scenarios when they can just start planning for these issues now. The news media, internet, and futures books have done a creditable job of outlining such mega issues as global warming, terrorism, and the like. Unfortunately, this is a misreading of the value of scenario-based planning. As Herman Kahn pointed out, the great benefit comes less in the prescriptive solution sets and more in the team-building aspects of the discovery process itself.[112] As long as all the parts of a whole system are engaged in a continuous dialogue, the entirety of the system will be infinitely better prepared to respond to both the immediate and the inevitable changes for the long term. Even practiced scenario-based planners acknowledge that their scenarios have a shelf life of only 3-5 years, beyond which they must be updated to account for the exponential growth of insights arising from new technologies, new discoveries, or curve balls thrown by Mother Nature. For those who think we have it all figured out, we would respectfully ask why we as a nation are so frequently surprised by world developments. The only solution is to to anticipate. This is the intent of scenario-based planning.

Cause 3b—Many believe that they do not need to build a common view of the future and find how they fit in the whole.

The idea of integration is not a widely held imperative across the whole of the U.S. Government as it is in the DoS and the DoD. Many departments believe they do not need to build a common view of the future and ascertain their place in it. They believe their missions are quite distinct, with the benefits of participating in a scenario to build a common awareness being problematic and uninspiring. Throughout the U.S. Government, departments looking to change culture struggle to recognize a need to integrate even within the same department. In some cases, the universal notion of integration may not be usefully applied in every instance. There may, in fact, be cases where systems do not meaningfully interact with other systems even within a single department. Within the Department of Commerce (DoC), for example, it is a stretch for the bureau on international sanctions to want to set up an integrated relationship with the oceanic and atmospheric folks on weathering and mapping. One can find some interconnections anywhere if one tries hard enough, but on the whole good critical analysis is a necessary prelude to dramatic wholesale solutions thrust upon a system. That said, if the exceptions are allowed to overshadow the entire argument of integration, as they are today, we will find this to be an unfortunate obstacle to an important aspect of the future. For we will experience more, not less, connectedness to one another as we progress into that future.

Cause 3c — Many lack the experience of operating as a team with those in other bureaus or departments.

Discounting the exceptional examples, where integration is unnecessary, many internal department cultures have never benefited from an experience where the blending of their own skill sets with those in other bureaus or in other departments could make the difference between failing and succeeding. The definition of what is success is at the root of this dilemma. Once success in major operations comes to be viewed as a whole rather the sum of its parts, then this challenge may be overcome.

Problem 4—The national security system rewards short-term results over long-term results.

The U.S. Government system is set up to focus on and reward the accomplishment of short-term results. This is evident in the practice whereby political appointees are hired every 4 years chiefly to carry out the immediate agenda of a President. Performance, then, is often measured in terms of starting or executing programs that most likely respond to the immediate political concerns of the day. Some would say long-term planning is even anti-democratic, forcing unwanted strategies made up by a previous administration to be binding on the next. These critics point out that the people's voices are exercised through the voting in of one administration in lieu of the previous administration, instantly dumping all past plans and policies except those explicitly chosen to be kept.

Cause 4a—The United States has always had a culture of the immediate.

The news media often reinforce this with its extensive 24-7 coverage of one crisis event after another rather than the long-term solutions. It might even be said that many poorer countries do *more* long-term thinking because they are family, tribal, or religion based. In those countries, maintaining continuity far into the future is an everyday endeavor, even if done so subconsciously. In America, the watchwords are change, speed, and competition. The American people revere their heroes today, but often revere even more tearing them down to replace them with the next objects of their infatuation. The "sound-bite" has become a staple in political life. Instant gratification is expected. Global warming may be the first major issue that has even begun to capture the truly long-term imagination of this or many other countries.

Cause 4b—The national security system has emphasized crisis management and neglected threat management.

Problem 5—Without means for matching resources to strategy, the national security system would be unable to act on scenario-based planning's insights for solution sets.

The way the government manages its resources (personnel, funding, etc.) prevents scenario-based planning from confidently producing practical and actionable insights leading to solutions. For example, the bifurcation of grand strategy between the office of Manpower and Budget and the National Security Council is cumbersome, resulting in disconnects between budget and strategy. Again, one could not imagine any successful business with such a separation between resources and strategies. The DoD is a fine example of an organization that can match resources to strategy, confident in using scenario-based planning as a tool for gaining the necessary insights into how to match these together in a responsible way.

3. *Consequence.*

The consequence of the national security system's lack of a core competence in strategic visioning is that the nation cannot identify strategic capabilities needed to deal with future threats and opportunities. Without a holistic vision, a system cannot articulate its ultimate purpose with clarity and granularity. Nor can it design its inputs (resources) and processes (methods) optimally to achieve its ultimate purpose. The lack of a common vision encourage the setting of incompatible goals, strategies, plans, and procedures across the U.S. National Security System.

CONCLUSION

This analysis considers the degree to which visions are developed across the U.S. Government and the extent to which those visions are or are not derived from scenario-based planning methodologies. The development of visions through the use of long-term scenario-based planning is limited, occuring primarily in the defense and intelligence communities. The majority of visions that are developed across the U.S. Government are not informed by scenario-based planning.

Without a holistic vision and mission, a system cannot satisfactorily articulate its ultimate purpose or the design of its inputs (resources) and processes (methods).

There is currently no established whole-of-government process and forum to enable the development of a common vision for the U.S. National Security system, the U.S. Government, or the nation. In addition to the absence of a government-wide vision, there is currently no overarching process, forum, or venue in which a vision could be developed. The development of such a vision would require a process, forum, and a venue that truly transcended departmental biases and perspectives. The only such forum that arguably exists today is the National Security Council (NSC) and its system of Policy Coordinating Committees (PCCs). The PCC system could provide a very rudimentary capacity to start a visioning process but to date this system has not been used to bring the government together for the purpose of visioning or planning. The PCC process is much more geared to the administration's daily inbox, short-term issues, and campaign goals. A much more robust, dedicated, and comprehensive capability is needed in the executive branch.

ENDNOTES-APPENDIX B

1. Edward Cornish, *Futuring: The Exploration of the Future,* Bethesda, MD: World Future Society, 2005.

2. *Ibid.*

3. Herman Kahn and Anthony Wiener, *The Year 2000: A Framework for Speculation on the Next Thirty-Three Years,* New York: Macmillan, 1967.

4. Kees Van der Heijden, "Articulating the business idea: the key to relevant scenarios," L. Fahey and R. Randall, eds., *Learning from the Future: Competitive Foresight Scenarios,* New York: John Wiley and Sons, 1998.

5. Finntrack, "Higher and Further Education Learning Contents," available from *finntrack.eu/management_centre/operations_and_supplychain.html.*

6. This section is adapted from a VWG literature review on *Organizational Scenario Use,* developed by Trudi Lang, Project on National Security Reform Working Paper, Washington, DC, 2008.

7. Kees Van der Heijden, *Scenarios: The Art of Strategic Conversation,* 2nd Ed., Chichester, UK: John Wiley & Sons, 2005.

8. Rene Zentner, "Scenarios, Past, Present and Future," *Long Range Planning,* Vol. 15, No. 3, 1982, pp. 12-20.

9. Kahn and Wiener, *The Year 2000.*

10. *Ibid.*

11. Fred Emery and Eric Trist, "The causal texture of organizational environments," *Human Relations,* Vol. 18, 1965, pp. 21-32.

12. *Ibid.*

13. Bood Robert and Theo Postma, "Strategic learning with scenarios," *European Management Journal,* Vol. 15, No. 6, 1997, pp. 633-647.

14. Stephen Millet, "The future of scenarios: challenges and opportunities," *Strategy & Leadership*, Vol. 31, No. 2, 2003, pp. 16-24.

15. Kees van der Heijden *et al.*, *The Sixth Sense: Accelerating Organizational Learning with Scenarios*, Chichester, UK: John Wiley and Sons, Ltd., 2002.

16. Robert Linneman and Harold Klein, "The Use of Multiple Scenarios by U.S. Industrial Companies," *Long Range Planning*, Vol. 12, 1979, pp. 83-90.

17. Pentti Malaska, Martti Malmivirta, and Sten-Olaf Hansen, "Scenarios in Europe—who uses them and why?" *Long Range Planning*, Vol. 17, No. 5, 1984, pp. 45-49.

18. Robert Linneman and Harold Klein, pp. 94-101.

19. Department of Homeland Security, "Strategic Plan: Securing Our Homeland," October 31, 2007, available from *www.dhs.gov/xabout/strategicplan/*.

20. Department of Treasury, "Strategic Plan: Fiscal Years 2007-2012," available from *www.ustreas.gov/offices/management/budget/strategic-plan/2007-2012/home.html#vision*.

21. Department of State and Agency for International Development, "Strategic Plan Fiscal Years 2007-2012," May 7, 2007, available from *www.state.gov/documents/organization/86291.pdf*.

22. Department of Defense, "Joint Vision 2020," available from *www.dtic.mil/jointvision/jvpub2.htm*.

23. Department of Justice, "Strategic Plan: Fiscal Years 2007-2012," available from *www.usdoj.gov/jmd/mps/strategic2007-2012/dojstrategicsummary.pdf*.

24. Department of Homeland Security, "Strategic Plan: Securing Our Homeland," October 31, 2007, available from *www.dhs.gov/xabout/strategicplan/*.

25. Department of Defense, "Joint Vision 2020," available from *www.dtic.mil/jointvision/jvpub2.htm.*

26. Department of State and Agency for International Development, "Strategic Plan Fiscal Years 2007-2012," May 7, 2007, available from *www.state.gov/documents/organization/86291.pdf.*

27. Department of Homeland Security, "Strategic Plan: Securing Our Homeland," October 31, 2007, available from *www.dhs.gov/xabout/strategicplan/.*

28. Department of Homeland Security, *DHS Releases National Preparedness Guidelines*, September, 2007.

29. *Ibid.*

30. Department of Justice, "Strategic Plan: Fiscal Years 2007-2012," available from *www.usdoj.gov/jmd/mps/strategic2007-2012/dojstrategicsummary.pdf.*

31. Department of Treasury, "Strategic Plan: Fiscal Years 2007-2012," available from *www.ustreas.gov/offices/management/budget/strategic-plan/2007-2012/home.html#vision.*

32. Department of Treasury, "Office of Performance Budgeting and Strategic Planning: Strategic Plan FY 2007-2012," September 19, 2007, available from *www.ustreas.gov/offices/management/budget/strategic-plan/.*

33. Department of Health and Human Services, "About Centers for Disease Control and Prevention," available from *www.cdc.gov/about/.*

34. Department of Health and Human Services, "Strategic Plan: Fiscal Years 2007-2012," October 31, 2007, available from *aspe.hhs.gov/hhsplan/2007/.*

35. Department of Agriculture, "About USDA," June 3, 2004, available from*www.usda.gov/wps/portal/!ut/p/_s.7_0_A/7_0_1OB?parentnav=ABOUT_USDA&navid=MISSION_STATEMENT&navtype=RT.*

36. Department of Energy, "Strategic Plan: 2006," available from *www.energy.gov/media/2006StrategicPlanSection4.pdf*.

37. Department of Energy, "About the Department of Energy," available from *www.energy.gov/about/strategicplan.htm*.

38. Office of the Director of National Intelligence, "Vision and Mission," December 13, 2007, available from *www.dni.gov/aboutODNI/mission.htm*.

39. Department of Labor, "Strategic Plan: Fiscal Years 2006-2011," December 13, 2007, available from *www.dol.gov/_sec/stratplan/strat_plan_2006-2011.htm#sg*.

40. Department of Commerce, "Bureau of Industry and Security," available from *www.bis.doc.gov/nectic/nec2.htm*.

41. Office of the Director of National Intelligence, "Vision and Mission," December 13, 2007, available from *www.dni.gov/aboutODNI/mission.htm*.

42. See *www.dni.gov/100-day-plan/100-day-plan.htm*.

43. See *www.dni.gov/500-day-plan/500-day-plan.htm*.

44. *Ibid*.

45. See *Defense Planning Scenarios*, Joint Experimentation, Transformation, and Concepts Division (JETCD), available from *www.dtic.mil/futurejointwarfare/dps.htm*.

46. *Joint Publication (JP) 5-0, Joint Operation Planning*, Washington, DC: Chairman, Joint Chiefs of Staff, 2006, p. xi.

47. *Ibid*.

48. *DHS Releases National Preparedness Guidelines*, Washington, DC: Department of Homeland Security, September 2007.

49. Department of Homeland Security, *National Planning Scenarios*, April 2005.

50. Office of the U.S. Director of National Intelligence public website, NIC Mission, available from *www.dni.gov/nic/NIC_about.html*.

51. Much of the information required to complete Appendix B has been validated using publicly available sources wherever possible. Selected information was obtained from internal government websites that are not available for routine public viewing. A current web address is provided wherever possible for the reader's review.

52. Office of the U.S. Director of National Intelligence public website, Vision and Mission, available from *www.odni.gov/aboutODNI/mission.htm*.

53. Office of the U.S. Director of National Intelligence public website, NIC Mission, available from *www.dni.gov/nic/NIC_about.html*.

54. Office of the U.S. Director of National Intelligence internal website, *www.odni.ic.gov*.

55. *Ibid.*

56. *Ibid.*

57. *Ibid.*

58. Office of the U.S. Director of National Intelligence public website, NIC Global Trends, available from *www.dni.gov/nic/special_globaltrends2010.html*.

59. Office of the U.S. Director of National Intelligence public website, NIC Global Trends, available from *www.dni.gov/nic/NIC_globaltrend2015.html*.

60. Office of the U.S. Director of National Intelligence public website, NIC Global Trends, available from *www.dni.gov/nic/NIC_2020_project.html*.

61. Global Futures Forum provides a password-protected yet publicly available website. The information referenced within this paper is available from *https://www.globalfuturesforum.org/Home.php*.

62. *Ibid.*

63. *Ibid.*

64. Defense Intelligence Agency, "This is DIA," available from *www.dia.mil/thisisdia/mission.htm*.

65. Interview with Ms. Lora Becker, Senior Advisor to the Deputy Under Secretary of Intelligence, Office of Intelligence and Analysis, U.S. Department of Homeland Security, April 23, 2008.

66. Interview with Ms. Deborah Barger, Assistant Deputy Under Secretary and Director of Policy, Strategy, and Doctrine Office, Deputy Under Secretary of Warfighter Support, Office of the Under Secretary of Defense for Intelligence, U.S. Department of Defense, April 21, 2008.

67. Briefing delivered by Mr. Patrick Gorman, Assistant Deputy Director of National Intelligence for Strategy, Plans, and Policy, Office of Policy, Plans, and Requirements, Office of the U.S. Director of National Intelligence.

68. *Ibid.*

69. *Ibid.*

70. Interviews with Assistant Deputy Director of National Intelligence Patrick Gorman and Assistant Deputy Under Secretary of Defense for Intelligence Deborah Barger.

71. Written input provided by Assistant Deputy Director of National Intelligence Patrick Gorman, April 20, 2008.

72. Written input provided by Ian Snyder, Director of Office of Strategy, Office of Strategy, Plans, and Policy, Office of Policy, Plans, and Requirements, Office of the U.S. Director of National Intelligence, April 23, 2008.

73. Interview with Assistant Deputy Under Secretary of Defense for Intelligence Deborah Barger, April 21, 2008.

74. Office of the U.S. Director of National Intelligence public website, Vision and Mission, available from *www.odni.gov/aboutODNI/mission.htm*.

75. Interview with Lora Becker, Senior Advisor to the Deputy Under Secretary of Intelligence, Office of Intelligence and Analysis, U.S. Department of Homeland Security, April 23, 2008.

76. *Ibid.*

77. Office of the U.S. Director of National Intelligence public website, Vision and Mission, available from *www.odni.gov/aboutODNI/mission.htm*.

78. Interview with Lora Becker, Senior Advisor to the Deputy Under Secretary of Intelligence, Office of Intelligence and Analysis, U.S. Department of Homeland Security, April 23, 2008.

79. This section is adapted from the IDA Draft Working Paper titled *The Military's Role in Conflict Prevention*.

80. *Project Horizon Progress Report*, Project Horizon, Summer 2006, p. 6, available from *www.osif.us/images/Project_Horizon_Progress_Report.pdf*.

81. *Ibid.*, p. 1.

82. *Ibid.*

83. *Ibid.*

84. *Ibid.*

85. See *Simulations*, United States Institute of Peace, available from *www.usip.org/class/simulations/*.

86. See *Professional Training*, United States Institute of Peace, available from *www.usip.org/training/dynamic/program_list.php?id=30*.

87. *IDA Research Summaries*, Vol. 7, No. 2, Fall 2000, p. 7, available from *www.ida.org/upload/research percent20notes/researchnotes-fall2000.pdf*.

88. *Simulation on Conflict Prevention in the Greater Horn of Africa*, United States Institute of Peace, undated, available from *www.usip.org/class/simulations/africa.pdf*.

89. See *African Union in a Nutshell*, African Union, available from *www.africa.-union.org/root/AboutAu/au_in_a_nutshell_en.htm*.

90. This section is adapted from the IDA Draft Working Paper: *The Military's Role in Conflict Prevention*.

91. *IDA Trip Report on Cornwallis XII conference*, IDA, 2007, p. 7.

92. Dr. Ted Woodcock, professor of Public Policy at George Mason University, is the primary developer of the STRATMAS.

93. *Senturion: Model Overview and Applications*, Sentia Group, 2006, PowerPoint presentation to the Institute for Defense Analyses, slide 2.

94. Developed by the Sentia Group, Senturion has been tested by the Center for Technology and National Security Policy (CTNSP) at the National Defense University (NDU) since 2002.

95. Based on IDA interview with Senturion developers, July 2006.

96. See *Synthetic Environments for Analysis and Simulation*, Simulex, available from *www.simulexinc.com/products/technology/*.

97. *IDA Trip Report on JFCOM/BENS Workshop*, IDA, June 2007, p. 6.

98. COMPOEX was jointly developed by the Defense Advanced Research Projects Agency (DARPA) and U.S. JFCOM.

99. See *POFED*, SENTIA Group, available from *sentiagroup.com/technology/pofed.asp*.

100. *Ibid.*

101. This section is adapted from the IDA Draft Working Paper titled *The Military's Role in Conflict Prevention.*

102. *Coalition Stability Operations (CSO) Project: First Working Group Meeting on Conflict Prevention, December 4-5, 2006, École Militaire, Paris, Meeting Report,* U.S. CREST, p. 4, available from *www.uscrest.org/070130_cso_ph2-1.pdf.*

103. *Ibid.*

104. *Ibid.*, pp. 5-6.

105. For key findings from this meeting, see *ibid.*, p. 23.

106. Press Briefing, "Exercise MILEX 07," European Union, June 2007, p. 2, available from *www.consilium.europa.eu/uedocs/cms_Data/docs/pressdata/en/esdp/94559.pdf.*

107. For more information on the Swedish role in MILEX 07, refer to Section 2 within Chapter II, Section C of accompanying paper: *The Military Role in Conflict Prevention Planning.*

108. Based on IDA interview with program director, July 2006.

109. See *Homepage*, Peace Team Forum, available from *www.fredsforum.se/eng/default_eng.htm.*

110. *Scenario Exercise: Cooperation in Prevention of Armed Conflict*, Peace Team Forum, 2006, p. 4, available from *www.fredsforum.se/PTF_Scenario_Exercise.pdf.*

111. United States, 2006, *National Security Strategy*, available from *www.whitehouse.gov/nsc/nss/2006/nss2006.pdf.*

112. Kahn and Anthony Wiener, *The Year 2000.*

ABOUT THE CONTRIBUTORS

SHEILA R. RONIS is Director of the MBA and Master of Management Programs at Walsh College. She is also President of The University Group, Inc., a management consulting firm and think tank specializing in strategic management, visioning, national security, and public policy. She teaches the "Strategic Management Capstone" course of the MBA, "Issues of Globalization" and "Strategic Management and Leadership" in the Doctorate of Management program at Walsh College. Dr. Ronis chairs the Vision Working Group of the Project on National Security Reform in Washington, DC, where she is responsible for the plan and processes to develop The Center for Strategic Analysis and Assessment, the venue where the President of the United States will conduct "grand strategy" on behalf of the nation. Dr. Ronis participates in many programs at the Industrial College of the Armed Forces (ICAF) at the National Defense University in Washington, DC including their National Security Strategy Exercise. In June 2005, she chaired at ICAF the Army's Eisenhower National Security Series Conference, "The State of the U.S. Industrial Base: National Security Implications in a World of Globalization." The *Proceedings* of that conference, which Dr. Ronis co-edited with Dr. Lynne Thompson, were published by the National Defense University Press in April, 2006. In March 2006, Dr. Ronis completed a study of the national security implications of the erosion of the U.S. industrial base for the U.S. House of Representatives Committee on Small Business. Her book, *Timelines into the Future: Strategic Visioning Methods for Government, Industry and Other Organizations,* was published by Hamilton Books in June 2007. She has authored nearly 200 articles and papers. Dr. Ronis holds a B.S. in physics and mathematics and an M.A. and Ph.D. from The Ohio State University where she studied large social system behavior.

LAUREN BATEMAN works for Senate Majority Leader Harry Reid on defense and foreign policy issues as a Legislative Correspondent. Formerly, she served as a research fellow for the Hudson Institute, and worked for the Project on National Security Reform (PNSR) Case Studies Working Group, where she authored a case study on the effect of Executive staffing transitions on the national security apparatus. She led a PNSR Interagency Reform roundtable discussion on the same topic. Ms. Bateman holds a B.A. from The College of William and Mary in history and government, where she focused on national security.

JIM BURKE is a Manager, Planner, and Senior Futures Analyst for TASC, Inc., where he is the head of the TASC Futures Group creating innovative studies of the future, emphasizing ways that early warning signals and trends can be exploited for business and government. He has over 25 years of experience in conducting futures and forecasting and has directed futures and change management efforts for a wide variety of government, nonprofit, and commercial clients, including Fortune 500 companies and foreign governments. Mr. Burke began his career in the Air Force where he was involved in operations, planning, and analysis of technologies, including industrial base assessments and technology for advanced systems (e.g., space, directed energy, stealth). Following his Air Force career, he worked for small and large companies doing technical program management, research, analysis, and technology forecasting, with a focus on industry technology trends. At TASC, Mr. Burke leads creativity, futures and forecasting/planning, and assessment sessions for commercial and government clients, including the National Institute of Standards and Technology on the future of intelligent machine technology, and the National Academies on reforming national security. In addition, he was involved in deep change management and organizational development based on technology advances for an intelligence agency. Mr. Burke has also led technical forecast and strategic assessments for an organization responsible for international telecommunications spectrum management, a complex effort to define strategic plans and innovative organizational approaches to emerging technologies. His nonprofit work covers the future of environmentalism, integrating renewable energy into state power portfolios, and sustainable development. He recently embarked on efforts to design social innovation approaches to blend profit and nonprofit ventures. Mr. Burke is a member of the American Society for Technology Innovation, the Association of Professional Futurists, and is a past president of the Washington, DC, chapter of the World Future Society. He holds a B.A. from the University of Detroit, an M.A. in Public Administration from the University of Northern Colorado, and an M.S. in science and technology studies from Virginia Tech.

CAYLAN FORD retains a strong research and advocacy interest in democratization, human rights, and civil society development in China. She is a master's degree candidate at the George Washington University's Elliott School of International Affairs where she concentrated in International Security

Policy. Ms. Ford completed her honors B.A. at the University of Calgary, where she focused her research on 20th-century Chinese history.

LEON FUERTH is the former National Security Advisor to Vice President Al Gore. Following 11 years as a Foreign Service Officer, Fuerth joined then-Congressman Gore's staff as senior legislative assistant for national security, focusing on issues of arms control and strategic stability. As the Vice President's National Security Advisor, Professor Fuerth served simultaneously on the Deputies' and Principals' Committees of the National Security Council, alongside the Secretary of State, the Secretary of Defense, and the President's own National Security Advisor. He created and managed five bi-national commissions, and led efforts to develop the International Space Station; to marshal international support for sanctions against Slobodan Milosevic's regime; to raise awareness of and take action to prevent the spread of HIV/AIDS in Africa; to denuclearize former Soviet states; to win China's cooperation in protecting the environment and reducing pollution; and to spur foreign investment in Egypt as part of the Middle East peace process. After retiring from government service at the conclusion of the Clinton administration, Professor Fuerth came to The George Washington University to serve as the J.B. and Maurice C. Shapiro Professor of International Affairs from January 2001 to January 2003. He currently serves as a research professor at the Elliott School of International Affairs and leads the Project on Forward Engagement, which incorporates three components: (1) a graduate seminar on long-range policy analysis; (2) expert seminars on unpacking Forward Engagement concepts; and (3) public outreach to U.S. citizens in an effort to create a constituency for apolitical long-range analysis and anticipatory governance. In addition, Professor Fuerth is currently a consultant for SCITOR, exploring use of space-based sensors in the design of a monitorable climate agreement; a member of the National Academy of Science Committee on Climate, Energy and National Security; a member of the Guiding Coalition for the Project on National Security Reform (PNSR); a consultant to The Alliance on Climate Change; and a consultant to former Vice President Al Gore. Professor Fuerth holds a bachelor's degree in English and a master's degree in history from New York University, as well as a master's degree in public administration from Harvard University.

LINDSEY GEHRIG contributed to the Nuclear Scenario during graduate school when she worked as a research fellow for the Project on National Security Reform. She currently works at the National Nuclear Security Administration in the Office of Nonproliferation and International Security. Ms. Gehrig lived in China for a year while focusing on learning Mandarin and teaching English at Shantou University. She holds a B.A. in politics from Whitman College and a master's degree in international affairs, with a concentration in U.S. foreign policy, from the School of International Service at American University in Washington, DC.

DANIEL LANGBERG is a professional researcher, writer, and analyst working on issues related to U.S. national security, foreign affairs, and homeland defense. He is a founding member of the Project on National Security Reform (PNSR) — a comprehensive effort to improve the U.S. Government's ability to meet the strategic challenges of the 21st century. He currently serves as Deputy Director for Interagency Teams and Planning and was recently the Deputy Director of the first-ever comprehensive study of the National Counterterrorism Center's Directorate of Strategic Operational Planning. Since 2005, Mr. Langberg has worked at the Institute for Defense Analyses (IDA) where he conducts research focused on complex contingencies and interagency affairs. At IDA, he published numerous studies and provided analytical support to the stand-up of the Department of State's Office of the Coordinator for Reconstruction and Stabilization and the U.S. military command in Africa (AFRICOM). Since 2004, Mr. Langberg has worked as a consultant for the United States Institute of Peace conducting in-country training and tutoring of Iraqi, Polish, and Moldovan government officials on the interactive computer simulation (Synthetic Environments for National Security Estimates— SENSE) modeling post-conflict societal transition and collaborative decisionmaking. Prior to his current positions, he worked in Washington, DC, at the Hudson Institute and in the Office of the Secretary of Defense for Networks and Information Integration. Mr. Langberg holds a bachelor's degree from the University of Pittsburgh and a master's degree in peace operations policy from George Mason University.

JAMES R. LOCHER III has worked in the White House, Pentagon, and Senate. He served as the senior staff member on the Senate Armed Services Committee for the Goldwater-Nichols Defense Reorganization Act and later for the Cohen-Nunn Amendment that created the U.S. Special Operations Command. In the first Bush and early Clinton administrations, Mr. Locher served as the assistant secretary of defense for special operations and low-intensity conflict. In 2003-04, he chaired the Defense Reform Commission in Bosnia and Herzegovina that successfully merged the three warring factions into a single military establishment and began the move toward a single army. Currently, Mr. Locher serves as the President and CEO of the nonpartisan Project on National Security Reform, which was established to assist the nation in reforming its national security system to meet the challenges of the 21st century. He is a graduate of West Point and Harvard Business School.

JOHN MEAGHER is a Senior Planner and Project Manager with the Futures Group at TASC, Inc., with expertise in industrial hygiene and environmental health/safety, futures analysis and strategic planning, risk assessment, international management systems, and homeland security. Mr. Meagher is also a Certified Industrial Hygienist with 26 years of experience in the occupational health and environmental science field. Currently, he is on assignment as the Executive Advisory Assistant to the Director of Basic and Applied Research for the U.S. Defense Threat Reduction Agency, where he provides senior level professional advice and support for all objectives to meet the directorate's goals of fostering and enabling farsighted, high payoff research focused on the unique challenges related to countering weapons of mass destruction (WMD). At TASC, Mr. Meagher has contributed to the development of methodologies for unconventional threat assessment and a historical study of radiological/nuclear threats for the Department of Homeland Security. He was the lead author of two industrial base studies for the Air Force on aerospace structural composites and managed a complex risk management and planning project for DoD's Missile Defense Agency. Currently, he is a contributor to George Washington University's Technological Forecasting Project, to the United Nations University Millennium Project focus groups on environmental issues and environmental consequences of war, and to the founding of the World Futures Network with the International World Future Society. As an independent consultant prior to joining TASC, Mr. Meagher provided expert legal scientific testimony and support, and business development and expertise to clients as an industrial hygienist and environmental health/safety scientist by providing unbiased, objective professional expertise in environmental health, occupational hygiene, analytical chemistry, and related public health sciences. At present, he is an adjunct assistant professor of occupational and environmental health and a guest lecturer regarding future study techniques at George Washington University. Mr. Meagher has published articles on homeland security, the future of industrial hygiene, and how futurists can assist decisionmaking. He is a professional member of the World Future Society and a past president of the Washington, DC, chapter of the World Future Society and the American Industrial Hygiene Association's Potomac (Washington DC, Northern VA, Maryland area) chapter. Mr. Meagher holds a B.S. in chemistry from Kent State University.

ROBERT B. POLK has served in various senior level planning and execution management positions both in and out of government. Today, he remains a Senior Adjunct Research Member and Consultant with the Institute for Defense Analyses in Washington, DC, where his on-going experience helped develop such capacity in several U.S. departments. He continues to provide valuable insights in that capacity. He recently completed 3 years as Senior Advisor, Strategic Planner, Deputy Issue Team Lead, and co-founding member of PNSR. Mr. Polk had a 20-year military career as both a front lines combat infantry officer and senior civil-military strategist for major Army and multi-service commands serving across the international spectrum from Thailand and Japan to Bosnia, Germany, and Iraq, including many months as the co-creator and Co-Director of the Office of Policy Planning in the United Nations-sanctioned Coalition Provisional Authority under Ambassador L. Paul Bremer in the early days of Iraq. Preceding this, Mr. Polk served as the Director of Plans for the original U.S. civil-military coordination team going into Baghdad (the Office of Reconstruction and Humanitarian Assistance led by Lieutenant General (Ret.) Jay Garner). Mr. Polk is a West Point graduate and holds three master's degrees including a Master of Military Arts and Science in Operational Theory and Strategic Planning from the Army's School of Advanced Military Studies, and a Master of Arts in National Security and Strategic Studies from the U.S. Naval War College.

MATTHEW RUSSELL is a senior Chinese military and defense analyst with the Futures Group at TASC, Inc. He has over 20 years experience in long-range planning and national security affairs. At TASC, Dr. Russell performs research and analysis of futures-oriented homeland security, defense, and technology issues. He has contributed to studies on the future of robotics for the National Institute of Standards and Technology, selected sectors of the aerospace industrial base for the U.S. Air Force, and nuclear terrorism and unconventional/emerging terrorist threats for the

Department of Homeland Security. Before coming to TASC, Dr. Russell was with SAIC, where he served as an on-site policy analyst for the U.S. Air Force Strategy and Policy division, leading studies on long-range Air Force strategy in East Asia and on future Chinese military developments. Prior to SAIC, he served in the Office of the Under Secretary of Defense for Policy as an assistant for long-range strategy development where he helped develop policies on future military technologies and capabilities, such as space-based surveillance systems, theater missile defense, information warfare, and the revolution in military affairs. Additionally, Dr. Russell prepared a study on future DoD hedging strategies against unanticipated future threats. Before joining DoD, he was an environmental and urban planner performing long-range planning studies for federal, regional, and local governments. Dr. Russell holds a B.A. in history from Northwestern University, an M.A. in history from the University of California-Davis, and an M.Phil. and Ph.D. in Chinese military history from George Washington University.

CHRISTOPHER WAYCHOFF is a Senior Project Manager and Strategic Analyst with the Futures Group at TASC, Inc., and has over 20 years of analytical and management experience specializing in bringing together interdisciplinary teams to develop innovative analytical studies, tools, and systems. He has experience in a broad range of technologies, methodologies, and organizations, particularly in technology and industrial base analysis, threat analysis, nuclear arms control, future trends analysis, and long-range strategic planning. At TASC, Mr. Waychoff developed quantitatively informed technology forecasts and scenarios for the future of robotics and artificial intelligence software for the automotive, aerospace, and construction industries for the National Institute of Standards and Technology. He was the technical lead in developing an emerging threat assessment center for the Department of Homeland Security and was senior analyst on a long-range competitive analysis, strategic plan, roadmap, and implementation plan for DoD's Joint Spectrum Center. In addition, he led a team drafting a DoD Analysis of Alternatives for a new spectrum management system and was a contributor to a senior-level study of the future of test, evaluation, and systems engineering for the DoD. Mr. Waychoff was also the business development lead for a science and technology management system, an automated supply chain vulnerability warning system, and a next generation strategic planning and future visioning center. From 1988 to 1995, Mr. Waychoff was project director and senior analyst at the U.S. Congress Office of Technology Assessment (OTA) in the International Security and Space Program. At OTA, he managed a multi-year assessment of the future space launch vehicle and long-range ballistic missile technology and industrial base. This study included technology forecasts, market structure analyses, competition projections, research and development funding priorities, and affordability assessments. At TASC, Mr. Waychoff authored *Supplier Partnerships in 2010: A DoD/Industry Vision* and co-authored *The Practical Guide to Integrating Acquisition and Logistics*. While at OTA, he authored numerous studies and reports, notably *The National Space Transportation Policy: Issues for Congress* and *The Lower Tiers of the Space Transportation Industrial Base*. Mr. Waychoff holds a B.A. in political science from the University of Pennsylvania and an M.A. in Soviet studies from Harvard University.